BIZARRE BOOKS

· · · · · · · ·

RUSSELL ASH
BRIAN LAKE

The LITTLE THROW=BACK
FIRE EXTINGUISHER

**GO ON READING
KEEP COOL———**

BIZARRE BOOKS

· · · · · · · · ·

RUSSELL ASH
BRIAN LAKE

PAVILION

First published in Great Britain in 1998 by
PAVILION BOOKS LTD
London House, Great Eastern Wharf
Parkgate Road, London SW11 4NQ

Text illustrations © Russell Ash and Brian Lake 1998
Cover photography by Angelo Homak © Pavilion Books Limited 1998

Designed by Bet Ayer

A CIP catalogue record for this book is available from the British Library

ISBN 1 86205 102 X

Set in Adobe Caslon

10 9 8 7 6 5 4 3 2 1

This book can be ordered direct from the publisher.
Please contact the Marketing Department. But try your bookshop first.

CONTENTS

INTRODUCTION

Let's get one thing straight to begin with: all the titles in
Bizarre Books are genuine. The authors either (a) own
a copy, (b) have seen a copy, or (c) have located a catalogue
entry for every book listed. We have excluded fabrications,
spoofs (I. M. Horny excepted) and contrived titles. We
make no apologies for including any book, but if any
sensitive author is distressed at being lampooned, we
ask forgiveness.

Bizarre Books was first published in 1985, in the age of
the wireless and the bowler hat. The entries were 'typed' onto
'index cards' and filed in boxes. The authors received many
'autograph letters' written in fountain pen from correspon-
dents, including long missives from expatriates dwelling in
the far-flung colonies of the British Empire.

How quaint that all seems today: this new edition,
stripped down, checked out on-line, expanded with the
help of e-mailed contributions from academics, librarians,
booksellers, collectors and other wired individuals, then
processed on a powerful computer, has been brought kicking
and screaming into a harsher, faster publishing world that
takes itself far too seriously – *vide* many of the new entries
from the last ten years or more.

Despite the new technology, *Bizarre Books* remains firmly rooted in the printed page. As well as our own serendipitous discoveries, many of the additions come from the army of readers and collectors who have an eye and ear for the inane and the insane, and the ability to pick out the bizarre from the bazaar of 150,000-odd (some extremely so) new books published every year in the English-speaking world alone. The Diagram Group Prize, awarded annually to the finder of the book that 'most outrageously exceeds all bounds of credibility', goes from strength to strength, its submissions now a familiar feature in *The Bookseller*, the weekly British book trade journal. *The Bookdealer* similarly organizes competitions for the most outlandish titles. Publishers have even proffered their own books, such is the kudos attached to winning such awards, while librarians in particular have jumped at the opportunity to submit entries to this new edition, and the nutty professors with personal collections, a mere handful a decade ago, have emerged *en masse* from their academic closets to become major contributors.

The genre is alive and well, but to keep it so, and to analyse which sections of the book are the most popular, we positively encourage the continuing involvement of our readers. Please send us your personal Top 10 entries from this new edition, with a note of your favourite sections, adding any titles you would like to see in the next edition – ideally, with documentary proof of their authenticity. You can write to us c/o the publishers, or e-mail us at ash@pavilion.co.uk.

Russell Ash, Lewes
Brian Lake, London

NOTES

All books are published in London unless otherwise stated.
Most chapters are arranged alphabetically by author.
n.d.: no date
n.p.: no publisher

1

THEY DIDN'T REALLY MEAN IT

Unintentional double-entendre *titles*

Women on the Job
Judith Buber Agassi
Lexington, Mass.: Lexington Books, 1979
A lively account of the activities of professional women.

The Resistance of Piles to Penetration
Russell V. Allin
Spon, 1935
An important treatise on a common problem.

Games You Can Play with Your Pussy
Ira Alterman
Watertown, Mass.: Ivory Tower Pub. Co., 1985

American Bottom Archaeology
Charles John Bareis and James Warren Porter
Chicago, Ill.: University of Illinois Press, 1983

How It Was Done at Stow School
Anon.
Hamilton Adams, 2nd edition, 1888
The author did not like the way it was done at all.

The Boy Fancier
Frank Townend Barton
Routledge; New York: E. P. Dutton, 1912
Tips on caring for domestic pets.

Enter Ye In
James Sidlow Baxter
Edinburgh: Marshall,
Morgan and Scott, 1939
And after twenty-one years:
Going Deeper
Edinburgh: Marshall,
Morgan and Scott, 1960

Couplings to the Khyber
Percy Stuart Attwood
Berridge
Newton Abbot: David and
Charles, 1969
Riveting tales of the
railways.

"Green Balls". The
Adventures of a Night
Bomber
Paul Bewsher
Edinburgh: W. Blackwood
and Sons, 1919

The Last Agony of the
Great Bore
F. W. Bird
Boston, Mass.: Dutton, 1868
On the drilling of the
Hoosac Tunnel.

The Saddle of Queens
Lida Louise Bloodgood
J. A. Allen, 1959

Enid Blyton's Gay Story
Book
Enid Blyton
Hodder and Stoughton, 1946
An unusual selection by the
queen of storytellers. The
stories include:
> The Three Sailors
> Let's Play Worms
> Dame Poke-Around
> That Tiresome Brownie

Persevering Dick
Mary D. R. Boyd
Philadelphia, Pa.:
Presbyterian Board of
Publication, 1867
Richard's dogged
determination does not
go unrewarded.

Ball Punching
Tom Carpenter
Athletic Publications, 1923
'World's Champion All-
round Ball-Puncher' – but
then balls usually are round,
aren't they?

Where to Say No
Rose Terry Cooke
Gall and Inglis, 1887
Miss Cooke lays down the law.

**The Garden of Ignorance.
The Experiences of a
Woman in a Garden**
Marion Cran
Herbert Jenkins, 1913
The author leads us up the garden path in this down to earth series:
The Garden of Experience
Herbert Jenkins, 1922
The Joy of the Ground
Herbert Jenkins, 1928
The Lusty Pal
Herbert Jenkins, 1930
The Story of my Ruin
Herbert Jenkins, 1924

**Flashes from the Welsh
Pulpit**
J. Gwnoro Davies (ed.)
Hodder and Stoughton, 1889
'...it is to be hoped that these Flashes have retained sufficient *heat* to warm some Christian's heart.'

Penetrating Wagner's Ring
John L. Di Gaetanao
New York: Da Capo, 1978
An in-depth study of the great composer's *Meisterwerk.*

The Pansy Books
Ida M. Loder Donisthorpe
*G. Routledge, 1887–90
(27 vols)*
A comprehensive library of pansiana.

**Men Who Have Risen:
A Book for Boys**
Charles Altamont Doyle
(illustrator)
J. S. Virtue, 1859

Fishing for Boys
J. H. Elliott
Harrap, 1961

Chaps and Short Pants
Herbert Farris
G. G. Swan, 1946

**Vince the Rebel; or,
Sanctuary in the Bog**
G. Manville Fenn
Chambers, 1897

Law Relating to Carriage of Goods by Sea in a Nutshell
Marston Garsia
Sweet and Maxwell, 2nd edition, 1925

Erections on Allotments
George W. Giles and Fred M. Osborn
Central Allotments Committee, n.d.

Whippings and Lashings
The Girl Guides Association, 1977
The anonymous author of this little gem (in both senses – it measures just 3 inches by 2.5 inches) offers some sound advice: 'Always use ropes or cord of suitable thickness', and 'Do not fumble or use fancy methods'. A copy in the authors' collection has been annotated by a previous owner, with the codes '• = I can do it', and 'X = I can't do it'.

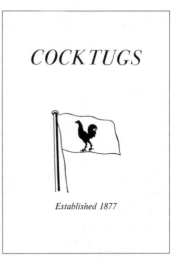

COCKTUGS

Established 1877

Cocktugs. A Short History of the Liverpool Screw Towing Company
W. B. Hallam
Liverpool: Printed by James Birchall and Sons, 1963

The Romance of Three Bachelors
Helen Harding
New York: n.p., c.1895

Kept for the Master's Use
F. R. Havergal
J. Nisbet, 1879

Making It in Leather
M. Vincent Hayes
New York: Drake, 1972;
Newton Abbot: David and
Charles, 1973
A how-to book for
devotees of this specialised
handicraft.

**Warfare in the Enemy's
Rear**
O. Heilbrunn
Allen and Unwin, 1963

**Handbook for the
Limbless**
Geoffrey Howson (ed.)
Disabled Society, 1922
With a foreword by John
Galsworthy.

**The Nature and Tendency
of Balls, Seriously and
Candidly Considered in
Two Sermons**
Jacob Ide
Dedham, 1818

**The Chronicles of the
Crutch**
Blanchard Jerrold
William Tinsley, 1860

The Tory Lover
Sarah Jewett
Smith, Elder, 1901

**Suggestive Thoughts for
Busy Workers**
J. Osborne Keen
*Bible Christian Book Room,
1883*

**Fanny's First; or, Tender
Trifles**
W. Brown Kitchiner
n.p., 1829

**The Big Problem of Small
Organs**
Alan T. Kitley
Colchester: The Author, 1966

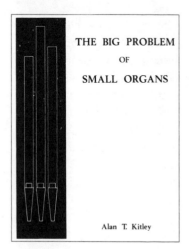

THE BIG PROBLEM
OF
SMALL ORGANS

Alan T. Kitley

A key difficulty solved in a noteworthy book.

'Having spent ten years devising schemes for the small organ I reluctantly decided that "there ain't no such animal", as a famous cowboy once said.' Mr Kitley then went away and wrote a book on it.

Explorations at Sodom
Melvin Grove Kyle
Religious Tract Society, 1928
Archaeological secrets uncovered.

Memorable Balls
James Laver
Derek Verschoyle, 1954
The eminent art historian recalls some fashionable Society entertainments.

Briefs Calmly Considered
'A Layman'
York: A. Barclay, 1826
The anonymous author is unaroused by his subject.

Shifts and Expedients of Camp Life
William Barry Lord and Thomas Baines
Horace Cox, 1871

The Midnight Cry; or, Signs in the Church of the Bridegroom's Second Coming
Rev. J. Lowes
Carlisle: n.p., 1800
A Sermon: 'Fire from Heaven… has burnt up our natural *heavens* of joy and delight in the flesh.'

Joyful Lays
Rev. R. Lowry and W. Howard Doane
New York and Chicago: Biglow and Main, 1886

Queer Doings in the Navy
Asa M. Mattice
Cambridge, Mass.: Line Officers' Association, 1896

School Experiences of a Fag at a Private and a Public School
George Melly
Smith, Elder, 1854

Little Lays for Little Lips
Helen J. A. Miles (illustrator)
William Wells Gardner, 3rd edition, 1875
Featuring 'The Foolish Chicken'.

Motor Cycles in a Nutshell
Swinfen Bramley Moore
P. Lund Humphries, 1923
Mr Moore was also the author of several other 'In a Nutshell' books including map-reading – a skill which he clearly lost when he wrote *Our Present Position: What About It?* (S. W. Partridge, 1922).

The Fags, and other Poems
William Moore
Kegan Paul, Trench, Trübner, 1912

British Tits
Christopher Perrins
Collins, 1979
A book to keep one abreast of ornithological knowledge.

The Oldest Trade in the World, and Other Addresses for the Younger Folk
George H. Morrison
Oliphant, Anderson and Ferrier, 1898
A title in the Golden Nails series.

Tinklings from the Sheepfolds
Matthias Pearson (pseudonym of John William Fletcher)
Simpkin, Marshall and Co., 1871
The author of *Flirtation; or, The Way into the Wilderness* (Robert Theobald, 1854) provides some interesting thoughts.

A Love Passage
Lady Harriet Phillimore
Christian Knowledge Society,
1908

Scouts in Bondage
Geoffrey Prout
Aldine Publishing Co., 1930

'Hurrah!' A Bit of Loving
Talk with Soldiers
Samuel Gillespie Prout
James Nisbet and Co., 1881

What Was Said in the
Woods
Gustav zu Putlitz
Longman, Brown, 1851

Report of the Committee
on Relations with Junior
Members
Oxford: Oxford University
Gazette, 1963

Shag the Caribou
C. Bernard Rutley
Macmillan, 1949
In the same series as *Peeko*
the Beaver, and not to be
confused with:

The Romance of the
Newfoundland Caribou
Arthur Radclyffe Dugmore
William Heinemann, 1913
or
Shag: Last of the Plains
Buffalo
Robert M. McClung
New York: Morrow, 1960
or even
Shag: The Story of a Dog
Thomas Clark Hinkle
Arrowsmith, 1932

Camping Among Cannibals
Alfred St Johnston
Macmillan, 1883
Dangerous exploits by an eccentric explorer.

The Comings of Cousin Ann
Emma Speed Sampson
Chicago, Ill.: Reilly and Lee Co., 1923

A French Letter Writing Guide
D. Sephton
Wicklewood: Primrose, 1980

Under Two Queens
John Huntley Skrine
Macmillan, 1884

The Scrubber Strategy
Robert T. Stafford
New York: Harper and Row, 1982

Fifty Years with the Rod
John Stirling
Philip Allan, 1929
An exhausting half-century described by the President of the Scottish Anglers' Association.

Betty Hyde's Lovers; or, The Household Brigade
Ralph Stone
n.p., c.1890

Invisible Dick
Frank Topham
D. C. Thomson and Co., 1926
' "Jeehosphat! What a disgraceful scene!" said Dick

Brett, doing a series of physical jerks behind a bush, as he began to grow into visibility.'

The Hooker's Art
Jessie A. Turbayne
Atglen, Pa.: Schiffer, 1993

Keeping your Tools Tiptop
Thomas Umpleby
Detroit, Mich.: The Author, 1954

The Gay Boys of Old Yale!
John Denison Vose
New Haven, Conn.: Hunter and Co., c.1869
Carefree varsity days recalled.

The Big Book of Busts
John L. Watson
San Francisco, Ca.: Hypermodern Press, 1994
A chess – rather than chest – book.

Organ Building for Amateurs
Mark Wicks
Ward Lock, 1887
A do-it-yourself guide to bigger and better organs.

Girls of the Pansy Patrol
May Wynne
Aldine Publishing Co., 1931
May Wynne was the pseudonym of Mabel Winifred Knowles, the author of over 200 girls' stories, including *Jill the Hostage* (Pearson, 1925) – a perfect partner for Geoffrey Prout's *Scouts in Bondage* (see page 17).

Eternal Wind
Sergei Zhemaeitis
Moscow: MIR, 1975

2

NAMES TO CONJURE WITH

Extraordinary authors' names

As with the rest of *Bizarre Books*, all the following authors' names are completely genuine and have been corroborated in the catalogues of the British Library and in the American National Union Catalog, and other authoritative sources. Inevitably, names such as Prick van Wily will be funnier to an English reader than to a Dutchman.

Pierre Anus
Istvan Apathy
Adeboye Babalóola
   (…bim bam boom?)
Gaspar Griswold Bacon
Pierre Jean Jacques
   Bacon-Tacon
Nellie Badcock
Ole Bagger
Marmaduke Baglehole
Ludwig von Baldass
Melville Balsillie [1]
Jean Baptiste Banal
Yoshimoto Banana
Rebecca Hammering Bang

Otto Banga [2]
Mrs Bleeker Bangs
Marmaduke Bannister
Ida Barney
Marston Bates [3]
Enrique Batty
Virgil L. Bedsole [4]
Forest Belt
Krista Bendová [5]
Rudyard Kipling Bent
Arngrim Berserk [6]
Myrtle Berry
Nicolas Bidet
Juana Bignozzi
René Palaprat de Bigot

Anthony Dung Bingel
Petr Bitsilli
Johanna Blows
Balthasar Blutfogel
Mody Coggin Boatright [7]
Maud Bodkin
Ion Bog
A. Bogie
Don Bolognese
Helen Knisely Bonk
Hugo Bonk
Kah-Ge-Ga-Gah-Bowh [8]
Wallop Brabazon
William Brassier
Melt Brink
Malte Brunk
Knud Bugge
Al Burt
Caspar Bussing
Perin H. Cabinetmaker
Desiré Carnel
Emu Ceka [9]
Eva Choung-Fux
A. Clot
Jacob Grubbe Cock
Bert de Cock
Levi Coffin
Ellsworth Prouty Conkle [10]
Hendrik Conscience
Ettrick Creak
Clement Crock
Lettice May Crump

Richard L. Daft [11]
Eugeniusz Dalek
Dee Day
T. Fox Decent
Mayhew Derryberry
Roger A. Destroyer
Robert Baby Buntin
    Dicebat [12]
Arsen Diklić
Ahn Doo-Soon
Kersi D. Doodha
Ugo Dotti
K. K. Douw Van Der Krap
Homer Hasenpflug Dubs
Ebenezer (5) Duty of
    Ohio [13]
Gottfried Egg
Bernt Eggen
Ekkehard Eggs
Gordon Bandy Enders
Jacob Fagot
Achilles Fang
Vera Fartash
A. Farto
Francis M. Fillerup
Gottfried Finger
Stuyvesant Fish
Hans Flasche
Mercedes Fórmica
Jessie Peabody Frothingham
Semen Frug
Stanka Fuckar

Martin Fucker
Clothilde Embree Funk
Brigitte Fux
Beowulf Gèobbel
Gergely Gergely
H. Roger Gobbel
Bess Goodykoontz
Colin Brummitt
   Goodykoontz
Biserka Grabar
B. Noice Grainger
Roland Grassberger
George L. Grassmuck
Arthur Grawehr-Butty
Wolf-Dietrich Grope
Janis Grots
Grub-dbang bKrashis
   rGyal-mtshan Dri-med
   sNying-po
Manfred Grunt
Romulus Guga
Serge Gut
Bernard Haggis
Billings Learned Hand
Odd Bang Hansen
Beatrice Harradan [14]
O. Heck
O. Hell
Burt Heywang [15]
J. Hogsflesh
Frederik Winkel Horn
Henriette Horny

Henry Hornyold-Strickland
Henry Beetle Hough
Herbert Hunger
Vincent Chukwuemeka Ike
Albert Irk
John Thomas Jeffcock
Oleh Kandyba
Jup Kastrati
Solon Toothaker Kimball
Kurt Kink
A. Kipper
Klaus Klang
Jèurgen Klapprott
Claudia Klodt
Onno Klopp
Verona Butzer Knisely
Bent Koch [16]
Hieronimus Knicker
Thorgny Ossian Bolivar
Napoleon Krok
Wolfgang Kunt
Johannes Kurzwelly
Joy Muchmore Lacey
Dirk La Cock
Roger Laprune
Faith B. Lasher
Herman von Lipps
Julius Lips
Tit Wing Lo
Roberto Haddock Lobo
Norbert Lohfink
P. van Loo

Bishop Lucifer of Cagliari
Georg Lunge [17]
Manfred Lurker
Jockey Mago
Ross Mangles
Marie Mauron
Patricia Pomboy Mintz
Voltaire Molesworth
Simon Young-Suck Moon
Professor A. Moron
Lucretia Coffin Mott
Rocco L. Motto
John Muckarsie
Bishop Frediricus Nausea
Endel Nirk
C. B. Noisy
Herbert Roof Northrup
Mildred Moody Nutter
Bishop Henry Ustick
    Onderdonk
Violet Organ
Pamela Balls Organista
P. C. Pant
Rene Perve
Polycarpe Poncelet
Fernando Poo
Mu-chou Poo
Malachy Postlethwayt
Harry Prick
Willy Prick
Willibald Psychyrembel
Ruth Rice Puffer

Harold Herman Punke
Mme J. J. Fouqueau de
    Pussy
Helmut Quack
Willem Quackelbeen
Maurice Rat
Camillo Ravioli
Hugh Ray
Hans Rectanus
Curt Redslob
Ferdinand William Risque
Valve Ristok
Margaret Cool Root
Hans Rotter
A. Schytte
James Patrick Sex
Abraham Shag
Willi Schmalz
I. I. Shitts
Helmit Sick
Markus Sickenberger
Mrs Hepsa Ely Silliman
Louis Sinner
Isidore Snapper
Ivor Snook
Ku Sok-pong
Negley King Teeters
Morten Thing
Nit Tongospit
Anna Ethel Twitt De Vere [18]
Baron Filiberto Vagina
    d'Emarese

Rolf Wank
Jessie Wee
Dr F. P. H. Prick
  van Wily [19]
Urban Grosskipper
  von Wipper [20]

Walter Womble
Ole Worm
Sabina Wurmbrand
Pedro Alid Zoppi

---

1. Author of *Let's Enjoy Ourselves* (The Cadet Supply Association, 1960).
2. Author of *Main Types of the Western Carotene Carrot and Their Origin* (Zwolle: W. E. J. Tjeenk Willink, 1963).
3. Author of *Man in Nature* (Englewood Cliff, NJ: Prentice Hall, 1961) and *Gluttons and Libertines: Human Problems of being Natural* (New York: Vintage Books, 1971).
4. Author of *A History of Western Civilization* (Baton Rouge, La.: Louisiana State University Press, 1936).
5. Author of *Čačky-hračky* (Bratislava: Mladé Letá, 1958).
6. Pseudonym of Olof von Dalin.
7. Co-author, with James F. Dobie, of *Straight Texas* (Austin, Tx.: Folk Lore Society of Texas, 1937).
8. Later changed his name to George Copway.
9. Pseudonym. His real name was F. Muck.
10. Author of *Crick Bottom Plays* (1928), *Poor Old Bongo* (1954), and *Son-of-a-Biscuit-Eater* (1958), all published in New York by Samuel French.
11. Author of *Understanding Management*, 1998.
12. His collected poems were published under the title, *Superman* (Constable, 1934).
13. The '(5)' appears as part of his name in the British Library catalogue.
14. Author of *In Varying Moods*, 1894.
15. Author of *Poultry Management in Subtropical, Semiarid Climates* (Washington, DC: United States Department of Agriculture, 1937).
16. Author of *Coryphoid Palm Fruits and Seeds from the Danian of Nāugssauq, West Greenland*, 1972.
17. Co-author with Ferdinand Hurter.
18. Inventor of a shorthand system.
19. Pseudonym.
20. Compiler of *Cassell's English–Dutch, Dutch–English Dictionary* (Cassell and Co., 1951).

3

THE RIGHT PERSON FOR THE JOB

Authors whose names are remarkably appropriate – or totally inappropriate – to the subjects of their books

Off the Cliff by Eileen Dover and *Twenty Years in the Saddle* by Major Bumsore are, of course, fictitious, but all those that follow are entirely genuine. In some instances, the authors share their names with celebrities, creating the improbable scenarios of Joan Collins, social worker, and an unmarried Elizabeth Taylor.

La Condition Sexuelle des Français
Henri Amoroso
Paris: Presses de France, 1963

The Cypress Garden
Jane Arbor
Mills and Boon, 1969

The Politics of Weapons Innovation
Michael Armacost
New York: Columbia University Press, 1969

Machine Tool Operation
Aaron H. Axelrod
New York: McGraw-Hill, 1941

Ballistics and Guided Missiles
A. Ball
Muller, 1960

Shy Men, Sex, and Castrating Women
Claude Balls
Trexlertown, Pa.: Polemic Press, 1985

A

TREATISE

O N

MADNESS.

By WILLIAM BATTIE M. D.

Fellow of the College of Phyſicians in LONDON,

And Phyſician to St. Luke's Hoſpital.

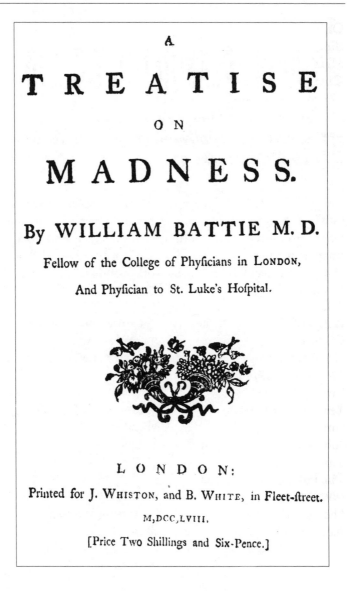

L O N D O N:

Printed for J. WHISTON, and B. WHITE, in Fleet-ſtreet.

M,DCC,LVIII.

[Price Two Shillings and Six-Pence.]

Organ Culture in Biomedical Research
Michael Balls
Cambridge University Press, 1976

Lead the Way Ladies!
Mrs M. A. Banger
Brighton: Brighton Herald, 1906

Punishment
Robin Banks
Harmondsworth: Penguin, 1972

A Treatise on Madness
William Battie
J. Whiston and B. White, 1758

Criminal Life: Reminiscences of Forty-Two Years as a Police Officer
Superintendent James Bent
Manchester: John Heywood, 1891
The original bent copper makes a full confession.

Winemaking with Canned and Dried Fruit
Cyril Berry
Andover: Amateur Winemaker, 1968

Les Classes Dirigeantes (The Ruling Classes)
Charles Bigot
Paris: Charpentier et Cie., 1875

Farm Poultry Raising
Herbert Roderick Bird
Washington, DC: United States Department of Agriculture, 1948

Surgical Diseases of the Chest
Brian Brewer Blades
St Louis, Mo.: Mosby, 1961

Put it in Writing
David Blot
Rowley, Mass.: Newbury House Publishers, 1980

Handbook of Lubrication
E. Richard Booser (ed.)
Boca Raton, Fla.: CRC, 1983–94

The Physical Dimensions of Consciousness
Edwin Garrigues Boring
New York: Century Co., 1933

Diseases of the Nervous System
Walter Russell Brain (Baron Brain)
Oxford: Oxford University Press, 1933

Home Wine-making
Harold Edwin Bravery
New York: Arco Publishing Co., 1968

Oh! Sex Education!
Mary Breasted
New York: Praeger Publishers, 1970

Food in Antiquity
Don and Patricia Brothwell
Thames and Hudson, 1969

Handbuch der Massage
Anton Bum
Berlin: Urban and Schwarzenberg, 1907

The Inner Flame
Clara Louise Burnham
Constable, 1912

Fruit Growing Outdoors
Raymond Bush
Faber and Faber, 1946

Discovering Bells and Bellringing
John Camp
Tring: Shire Publications, 1968

Le Nouveau Livre de Cuisine
Blanche Caramel
Paris: n.p., 1928

Motorcycling for Beginners
Geoff Carless
East Ardsley: EP Publishing, 1980

La Libertine
Nonce Casanova
Amiens: E. Malfère, 1921

The Abel Coincidence
J. N. Chance
Robert Hale, 1969

The Preacher; or, The Art and Method of Preaching
W. Chappell
Edward Farnham, 1656

Your Teeth
John Chipping
Cottrell and Co., 1967

Oppositions of Religious Doctrines
William A. Christian
Macmillan, 1972

A Musical Offering
Edward H. Clinkscale
New York: Pendragon Press, 1977

Every Other Inch a Methodist
Douglas J. Cock
Epworth Press, 1987

The Long Thirst: Prohibition in America, 1920–1933
Thomas M. Coffey
New York: Norton, 1975

**Death in Early America:
The History and Folklore
of Customs and
Superstitions of Early
Medicine, Funerals, Burial
and Mournings**
Margaret Coffin
*New York: E. P. Dutton,
1976*

**A New Look at Social
Work**
Joan Collins
Pitman, 1967

**Some Examples of Wave
Motion in Fluids**
Gordon David Crapper
*Liverpool: Liverpool
University Press, 1975*

**Predicting the Child's
Development**
W. F. Dearborn
*Cambridge, Mass.: Sci-Art
Publishers, 1941*

Inside Story
A. Dick
Allen and Unwin, 1943

Violence Against Wives
Emerson and Russell
Dobash
*Shepton Mallet: Open Books,
1980*

**A Primer of the Art of
Massage (For Learners)**
Dr. Stretch Dowse
8th edition, illustrated
*Bristol: John Wright and
Sons, 1892*

Textile Fabrics
Elizabeth Dyer
*Boston: Houghton Mifflin,
1923*

**Fundamentals of Arctic
and Cold Weather
Medicine and Dentistry**
Harry Belleville Eisberg
*Washington, DC: Research
Division, Bureau of Medicine
and Surgery, 1949*

Writing with Power
Peter Elbow
*Oxford: Oxford University
Press, 1981*

How to Live to a Hundred Years or More
George Fasting
New York: The Author, 1927

The Boy's Own Aquarium
Frank Finn
Country Life and George Newnes, 1922

A Bibliography of Water Pollution and Its Control
Hugh Fish
Henley-on-Thames: Gothard House, 1972

Sewage Treatment and Disposal
G. M. Flood
Blackie, 1926

The Roots of the Ego. A Phenomenology of Dynamics and of Structure
Dr Frankenstein
Baltimore, Md.: Williams and Wilkins, 1966

Sexual Desire and Love
Eric Fuchs
Cambridge: J. Clarke, 1983

Round the Bend in the Stream
Sir Wilmot Hudson Fysh
Sydney: Angus and Robertson, 1968

Common Truths from Queer Texts
Rev. Joseph Gay
Arthur Stockwell, 1908

Vasectomy: The Male Sterilization Operation
Paul J. Gillette
New York: Paperback Library, 1972

The Bog People
P. V. Glob
Faber and Faber, 1969

The Encyclopaedia of Association Football
Maurice Golesworthy
Robert Hale, 1967

Illustrated History of Gymnastics
John Goodbody
Stanley Paul, 1983

Running Duck
Paula Gosling
Pan Books, 1979

A Primer of Gross Pathology
William I. Grossman
Springfield, Ill.: Thomas, 1972

The Perfect Lawn
Roger Grounds
Ward Lock, 1974

Discovering Horn
Paula Hardwick
Lutterworth, 1981

Handbook of Trees, Shrubs and Roses
Walter Gordon Hazlewood
Sydney: Angus and Robertson, 2nd edition, 1968

The High Rise
Leo Heaps
W. H. Allen, 1972

An Introduction to Prehistoric Archaeology
Frank Hole
New York: Holt, Rinehart and Winston, 3rd edition, 1973

Industrial Social Security in the South
Robin Hood
Chapel Hill, NC: The University of North Carolina Press, 1936

An Essay on the Rupture called Hydrocele
Benjamin Humpage
Murray, 1788

Chess Pieces
Norman Knight
Sutton Coldfield: Chess, 1968

Lashing and Securing of Deck Cargoes
Captain John Knott
Nautical Institute, 1994

From the Deathbed to Boisterous Health
Morris Krok
Durban: Essence of Health, 1963

International Dairy Situation and Outlook
W. Krostitz
Rome: FAO, 1976
Krostitz is described as a member of 'The Milk and Milk Products Team'.

The Home Book of Turkish Cookery
Venice Lamb
Faber and Faber, 1969

Obesity: Causes, Consequences, and Treatment
Louis Lasagna
New York: Medcom Press, 1974

New and Rare Inventions of Water-Works
John Leak (translator)
Joseph Moxon, 1659

British Electric Trains
H. W. A. Linecar
Ian Allan, 1947

Of Such Is the Kingdom: A Nativity Play
Gladys Littlechild
Methuen, 1952

Anatomy of the Brain
William W. Looney
Philadelphia, Pa.: F. A. Davis, 2nd edition, 1932

The Grace of God
A. Lord
Truro: James R. Netherton, 1859

About Raw Juices
John B. Lust
New York: Benedict Lust Publications, 1982

Crocheting Novelty Pot-holders
L. Macho
New York: Dover, 1982

When I was a Boy; or, She Touched the Right Chord
Maria Manley
William Macintosh, 1864

Metabolic Changes Induced by Alcohol
G. A. Martini
Berlin: Springer-Verlag, 1971

Care for Your Kitten
Anna Mews
Collins, 1986

Riches and Poverty
L. G. Chiozza Money
Methuen, 1905

Salmon: The World's Most Harassed Fish
Anthony Netboy
Tulsa, Okla.: Winchester Press, 1980

Researches in Binocular Vision
Kenneth Neil Ogle
Philadelphia, Pa.: W. B. Saunders, 1950

The Lord's Supper
William Gilbert Ovens
Church Association, 1940

The Flood and Noah's Ark
A. Parrot
SCM Press, 1955

Spices from the Lord's Garden
Rev. E. I. D. Pepper
West Conshohocken, Pa.: n.p., 1895

Land Speed Record. A Complete History of the Record-breaking Cars from 39 to 600+ mph
Cyril Posthumus
Reading: Osprey, 1971

Marine Diesel Engines
C. C. Pounder
George Newnes, 1952

The Arena of Masculinity: Sports, Homosexuality, and the Meaning of Sex
Brian Pronger
New York: St Martin's Press, 1990

Nutrition and Diet Therapy
Fairfax Throckmorton Proudfit
New York: Macmillan, 7th edition, 1938

The Trimming and Finishing of Hosiery and Hosiery Fabrics
J. H. Quilter
Bradford: C. Greening, 1889

The Prevention of Juvenile Delinquency
Walter Cade Reckless
Columbus, Ohio: Ohio State University Press, 1972

A-Saddle in the Wild West
William Henry Rideing
J. C. Nimmo, 1879

Women and the Crisis in Sex Hormones
Barbara Seaman and Gideon Seaman
Hassocks: Harvester Press, 1978

Workshop Technology for Mechanical Engineering Technicians
C. R. Shotbolt
Cassell, 1971

By Reef and Shoal
William Sinker
Christian Knowledge Society, 1904

Lifeblood
Frank Gill Slaughter
New York: Doubleday, 1974
Slaughter was also the author of:
The Healer
Jarrolds, 1955
and
That None Should Die
Hutchinson, 1975

The Skipper's Secret
Robert Smellie
Edinburgh: D. M. Small, 1898

Voluntary Euthanasia: Experts Debate the Right to Die
Barbara Smoker
Peter Owen, 1985

Price Expectations and the Behaviour of the Price Level
R. Solow
Manchester: Manchester University Press, 1970

Electronics for Schools
R. A. Sparkes
Hutchinson Educational, 1972

In Quest of Quiet: Meeting the Menace of Noise Pollution
Henry Still
Harrisburg, Pa.: Stackpole Books, 1970

Abnormal Psychology: Understanding Behavior Disorders
Jack Roy Strange
New York: McGraw-Hill, 1965

Crime and Law
Adrienne P. Swindells
Hart-Davis, 1977
Swindells was also the author of *Running a Disco, Drugs* and *Throwing a Party* – all Hart-Davis, 1978.

Meditations of an Old Maid
Elizabeth Taylor
Cincinnati, Ohio: n.p., c.1900

The Evolution of Insect Mating Systems
Randy Thornhill and John Alcock

Cambridge, Mass.: Harvard University Press, 1985

The Imperial Animal
Lionel Tiger and Robin Fox
Secker and Warburg, 1972

La Formation de la Jeunesse
Désiré Tits
Bruxelles: Office de Publicité, 1945

Operation Earth
B. Trench
Neville Spearman, 1969

The Eighth Passenger
Miles Tripp
Heinemann, 1969

There Are No Problem Horses, Only Problem Riders
Mary Twelveponies
Boston, Mass.: Houghton Mifflin, 1982

Rope
William Tyson
Wheatland Journals, 1968

Winemaking: From Grape Growing to Marketplace
Richard P. Vine
New York: Chapman and Hall, 1997

Fuel Oil Viscosity-Temperature Diagram
Guysbert B. Vroom
New York: Simmons-Boardman, 1926

Nous and Logos: Philosophical Foundations of Hannah Arendt's Political Theory
William Paul Wanker
New York: Garland, 1991

Underground Jerusalem
Sir Charles Warren
R. Bentley and Son, 1876

Procedures for Salvage of Water-Damaged Library Materials
Peter Waters
Washington, DC: Library of Congress, 1975

The Principles of Insect Physiology
Vincent Brian Wigglesworth
Methuen, 1939

Natural History of Birds
Leonard William Wing
New York: Ronald Press Co., 1956

The World of My Books
I. M. Wise
Cincinnati, Ohio: American Jewish Archives, 1954

SPINE TITLES

Abbreviating authors' names and titles to make them fit on the spine of a book sometimes produces curious results. Some of them work best when recited aloud:

The Rectum
Sir Charles Bent Ball, *Ball on the Rectum*
Hodder and Stoughton, 1908

Gotobed on Darts
Jabez Gotobed, *Darts: Fifty Ways to Play the Game*
Cambridge: Oleander, 1980

Hogg on Sheep
James Hogg, *The Shepherd's Guide: being a Practical Treatise on the Diseases of Sheep*
Edinburgh: Archibald Constable, 1807

The Horse's Foot
William Miles, *Miles on The Horse's Foot*
Longman, 1846

Phar–Q–R–Salse
Century Dictionary, Vol. VI, *1899*

R–Soh
Grove's Dictionary of Music and Musicians
Macmillan, 1960

Tredd on Dice
William Evan Tredd, *Dice Games New and Old*
Cambridge: Oleander, 1981

Watts on the Mind
Isaac Watts, *The Improvement of the Mind*
Printed for J. Brackstone, 1741

Withering's Botany
William Withering,
A Botanical Arrangement of British Plants
Birmingham: Printed by M. Swinney, 1776

4

A MUSICAL INTERLUDE

Suggestions for an offbeat soirée

This selection represents a small sample from the vast collection of sheet-music titles in the British Library. Since the identity of a number of their authors is unknown, they are arranged alphabetically by title.

Art' Coming?
Leo Kerbusch, 1860
The song begins 'Deeper and deeper'.

Aspirations of Youth
Marcus Hast, 1874
The song begins, 'Higher, Higher'.

Ballads for Babies, with Merry Movements
Jennett Humphreys, 1888

Ball Tossing
H. Lottner, 1894

Beware my Fanny
John S. Geldard, c.1820
'Behold! my Fanny, yonder
    flow'r
How droops its lovely head –
It blows, and yet another
    hour
It withers and is dead.'

The Blind Boy
C. Cibber, 1874
The song begins, 'Oh! say
what is that thing?'

The Blind Boy
Kate Fanny Loder, 1873
The song begins, 'I feel with
delight'.

**Both Old Men and Young;
or, The Well Dispos'd
Organ Blower**
Anon., c.1730

Camping
Alec Rowley, 1928
In the *When I'm a Man*
series.

Come Before Mother is Up
Edward Cympson (pseudo-
nym of E. Sibson), 1876

Dance of the Rubber Dolls
Paul La Valle, 1919

**The Faggot-binders'
Chorus**
Anon., n.d.

Fair Cloris in a Pigstye Lay
'By a Welch Gentleman',
c.1720

Fairy-Fingered Fanny
Alfred E. Aarons, n.d.

The Fairy's Ball
Edith Dick, 1924

Fixed in His Everlasting Seat
Georg Friedrich Haendel, 1899

A Frenchman's Letter to His English Mistress
Anon., 1752

Galloping Dick
Percy Fletcher and G. Rothery, 1911

Gay Go Up
R. H. Walther, n.d.

The Gay Photographer
G. Grossmith, n.d.

A Handy Little Thing to Have About You
Harold Montague, n.d.

Hard at First; or, I'm a Daddy At It Now
Norton Atkins, 1894

I'd Tell You if I Were a Little Fly
Augustus Leach, 1877

I'll Place It in the Hands of My Solicitor
F. Gilbert, 1887

I Love Little Pussy
H. Farmer, n.d.

I Love Little Willie
John Jacob Niles, 1955
'To be sung in a gay, mocking manner'.

I Love My Love in the Morning
J. K. D. Bedwell, n.d.

I'm a Very Potent Queen
Georg Jacobi and L. H. F. de Terreaux, 1873

In the Depths of the Sea
T. T. Peed, n.d.

In Vain I Strive with Aspect Gay; or, Up all Night
Matthew Peter King, n.d.

I Smote Him on the Boko with My Whangee
William Hyde, n.d.

It's Really Quite Hard
Anon., 1899
The song begins, 'It's apt to be embarrassing'.

I Was Holding My Cocoanut
Charles Collins and J. Burley, n.d.

I Wasn't a Bit Like a Boy
E. Solomon, n.d.

I Won't be a Nun
Countess W-N-K, n.d.

The Joy-inspiring Horn
R. Bride, n.d.

Kornblumen
F. Arter, 1854

The Lapful of Nuts
Alicia Adelaide Needham, 1914

A Large Cold Bottle and a Small Hot Bird
John A. Stromberg, 1898

Let Me Hold It Till I Die
H. Lovegrove, 1864

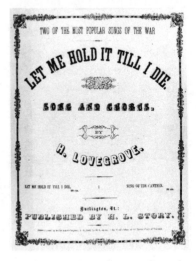

Let Us Be Gay
George Linley, c.1835
A favourite song in the musical drama of 'The Queen and the Cardinal'.

Loo Galop and Loo Waltz
J. Frascati, 1875
'Played nightly at the Strand Theatre'.

Love and a Bumper; or, Fanny's Delight; or, Come Sweet Lass
Anon., c.1750

The Man with the Four Point Seven!
Gaston de Breville, 1912

The Medical Wife
'F. I.', 1871
The song begins, 'I'm the queerest of husbands'.

Miniwanka; or, the Moments of the Water
Robert M. Schafer, 1973

The Monks Were Jolly Boys
From the operetta, 'Once Too Often' by Howard Glover, 1862

The Mumps
Mana Zucca, 1934

My Coon is a Lobster
Arthur Dunn, 1899

My Nancy Loves me Truly. An Agricultural Lay
W. Yardley, 1883

The Nobility Balls Polka
Anon., 1844
'With military band parts.'

No More Fancy Balls for Me
N. Atkins and Herbert Darnley, n.d.
'No more fancy balls for me!
They suit the aristocracy
   and parsons;
But if I have to go to any
   more balls
It'll be the old three brass
   'uns.'

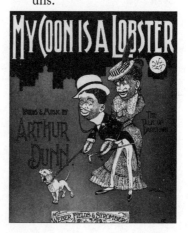

Open Thy Lattice, Darling!
G. H. Newcombe, 1890

Saw Ye My Wee Thing?
Anon., c.1796

Say Mama, If He Pops Shall I Send Him to You?
Henry S. Leigh, 1874

A Sea Side Lay
C. L. Kenney, 1882

The Snail's Galop
E. de Gremont, 1867

Sweet Dangle, Pride of Erin
E. Ransford, 1870

They've All Got Sticky Backs
J. W. Knowles, 1903

Uncle John, the Lay of the Hopeful Nephew
Henry S. Leigh, 1870

Wanderin' Willie; or, Here Awa', There Awa'
W. Moodie, 1902

When War's Alarms Entic'd My Willy from Me
T. Linley, c.1770

With My Little Wigger-wagger in My Hand
F. Earle, Frank Carter and Gilbert Wells, 1909

Ye Nymphs of Bath Prepare the Lay; or, On Princess Amelia
Maurice Greene, 1737

Yielding Fanny
Anon., c.1750

You Do Keep Popping In and Out
Albert Hall and J. W. Knowles, 1904

The Young Nun
Augusto Rotoli, 1884
The song begins 'When from above I seek relief'.

You're Getting It Up for Me
Augustus Leach, 1878

5

WE HAVE A BOOK ON IT

Astonishingly specialized subjects

The Turkish Bath: an Antidote for the Cravings of the Drunkard
A., J.
Dublin: R. D. Webb, 1859

The Care of Raw Hide Drop Box Loom Pickers
Anon.
Saco, Me.: Garland Manufacturing Co., 1922

Laundry Lists with Detachable Counter-checks in French, Spanish, Portuguese, German, Italian, Including Vocabularies and Necessary Phrases and Phonetic Spelling
Anon.,
Eyre and Spottiswoode, 1909

Octogenarian Teetotalers, with One Hundred and Thirteen Portraits
Anon.
National Temperance League Publication Depot, 1897
First the 'Unique Reception' in the Town Hall of St Martin's-in-the-Fields on 21 May 1896, and now the book!

Why People Move
Jorge Balan (ed.)
Paris: UNESCO, 1981

Der Begriff 'Silly Fool' im Slang einer Englischen Schule
H. Beck
Bern: Francke Verlag, 1982

The Development of a Procedure for Eliciting Information from Boys about the Nature and Extent of their Stealing
William Albert Belson, G. L. Millerson and P. J. Didcott
London School of Economics, n.d.

Organizing Deviance
Joel Best and David F. Luckenbill
Englewood Cliffs, NJ: Prentice-Hall, 1982

Shoe Bottom Costing
E. S. Bream
The British Boot, Shoe and Allied Trades Research Association, 1936

The Effect of Relative Humidity on an Oak-tanned Leather Belt
W. W. Bird
New York: American Society of Mechanical Engineers, 1915

The Line of Cleavage under Elizabeth
Dom Norbert Birt
Catholic Truth Society, 1909

Do Tables Tip?
James Black
Montreal: n.p., 1922

Specifications for Billets for Picking Sticks for Underpick Looms
British Standards Institution
BSI, 1965

Practical Candle Burning
Raymond Buckland
St Paul, Minn., Llewellyn Publications, 1970

Sodomy and the Pirate Tradition: English Sea Rovers in the Seventeenth Century Caribbean
Barry Richard Burg
New York: New York University Press, 1985

Selected Themes and
Icons from Spanish
Literature: Of Beards,
Shoes, Cucumbers, and
Leprosy
John R. Burt
*Madrid: José Porrúa
Turanzas, 1982*

A Glowing and Graphic
Description of the Great
Hole
Mrs D. U. C.
*Syracuse, NY: Daily Democrat
Office, 1848*

Timber-Framed Buildings
in Watford
S. A. Castle
Chichester: Phillimore, 1977

Jaws and Teeth of Ancient
Hawaiians
H. G. Chappel
*Honolulu: Honolulu Museum,
1927*

The History of the Self-
winding Watch, 1770–1931
Alfred Chapuis and Eugène
Jaquet
Batsford, 1952

Faith, Reason and The
Plague in Seventeenth
Century Tuscany
Carlo Cipolla
*Hassocks: Harvester Press,
1979*

Truncheons: Their
Romance and Reality
Erland Fenn Clark
Herbert Jenkins, 1935
With over 100 plates
illustrating more than 500
truncheons.

The Foul and the Fragrant:
Odor and the French
Social Imagination
Alain Corbin
*Cambridge, Mass.: Harvard
University Press, 1986*

Wall-Paintings by Snake
Charmers in Tanganyika
Hans Cory
Faber and Faber, 1953

Barbs, Prongs, Points, Prickers, and Stickers: A Complete and Illustrated Catalogue of Antique Barbed Wire
Robert T. Clifton
Norman: University of Oklahoma Press, 1970

Other books on barbed wire include:

Who's Who in Barbed Wire
Anon.
Texline, Tx.: Rabbit Ear Publishing Co., 1970
Containing 'Names and addresses of active barbed wire collectors'
and
The 'Bobbed' Wire III Bible
Jack Glover

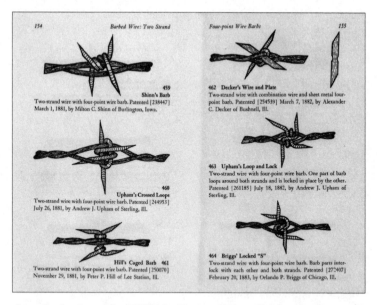

A small selection of the 992 **Barbs, Prongs, Points, Prickers, and Stickers**.

Sunset, Tex.: Cow Puddle Press, 1972
The definitive 'Centennial' edition of *'Bobbed' Wire* (1966). Glover was also the author of *The Sex Life of the American Indian*, 1968 and

Jesse James
Early United States Barbed Wire Patents
Maywood, Ca.: The Author, 1966

Anthropometric Measurement of Brazilian Feet
Mario P. D'Angelo and Delfina Falcao
Manchester: Manchester Metropolitan University, 1993

Paintings and Drawings on the Backs of National Gallery Pictures
Martin Davies
National Gallery, 1946

Moles and their Meaning. With regard to the Mind, Morals and Astral

Indications in Both Sexes, Being a Modernised and Easy Guide to the Ancient Science of Divination by the Moles of the Human Body (Founded on the Works and Researches of one Richard Sanders, A.D. 1653, and Other Eminent Astrologers of About the Same Period)
Harry de Windt
C. Arthur Pearson, 1907
The definitive work on moleosophy.

Male Infibulation
Eric John Dingwall
John Bale, Sons and Danielsson, 1925

The History of the Concrete Roofing Tile: Its Origin and Development in Germany
Charles Dobson
B. T. Batsford, 1959
'This book has been compiled with the single aim of interesting those who may like to learn something more about the

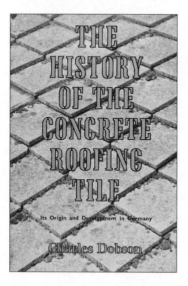

origin and development of the concrete roofing tile than is generally known in England.'

Crockery washing: the report of an investigation into crockery washing carried out for the Catering Advisory Service of the King's Fund with particular reference to the use of detergent dispensers and the centralisation of patient's [sic] crockery washing
King's Edward's Hospital Fund for London, 1967

How to Save a Big Ship From Sinking, Even Though Torpedoed
Charles V. A. Eley
Simpkin, Marshall and Co., 1915
The cover illustration shows a ship in a vertical position. It turns out to be the *Titanic*. The caption inside reads: 'And she did eventually attain the perpendicular'.

Canadian National Egg Laying Contests
F. C. Elford and A. G. Taylor
Ottawa: Department of Agriculture, 1924
Covers only the most interesting period, from 1919–22; after this, helium took off as the national obsession (see page 60).

The Social History of the Machine Gun
John Ellis
New York: Pantheon Books, 1975

European Spoons Before 1700
John Emery
John Donald, 1976

The Almost Complete Eclectic Caver
Thom Engel
Schohavie, NY: Speleobooks, 1992

Camel Brands and Graffiti from Iraq, Syria, Jordan, Iran and Arabia
Henry Field
Baltimore, Md.: American Oriental Association, 1952

Skeletal Remains of the Central Eskimos
Knud Ejvind Fischer-Møller
Copenhagen: Gyldendalske Boghandel, 1937

Also and Too: A Corpus-based Study of Their Frequency and Use in Modern English
B. Fjelkestam-Nilsson
Stockholm: Almqvist and Wiksell, 1983

The Needle on Full: Lesbian Feminist Science Fiction
Caroline Forbes
Onlywomen Press, 1985

Intemperance and Tight Lacing, Considered in Relation to the Laws of Life
O. S. Fowler
J. Watson; Wortley: Printed by Joseph Barker, 1849
'Total abstinence, or no husbands – natural waists, or no wives.'
'Let the finger of scorn be pointed at every tight-laced woman, and let tight waists be shunned... The practice is disgraceful, is immoral, is *murderous*; for it is gradual *suicide*, and almost certain *infanticide*.'

Prehistoric Sandals from Northeastern Arizona
Kelley Ann Hays-Gilpin, Ann Cordy Deegan, and Elizabeth Ann Morris
Tucson, Ariz.: University of Arizona Press, 1998

Scalping in America
Walter Hough
Mattituck, NJ: Amereon House, 1988

Multi-Armed Bandit Allocation Indices
John C. Gittins
Chichester: Wiley, 1989

Honor and Slavery: Lies, Duels, Noses, Masks, Dressing as a Woman, Gifts, Strangers, Humanitarianism, Death, Slave Rebellions, the Proslavery Argument, Baseball, Hunting, and Gambling in the Old South
Kenneth S. 'Have I Left Anything Out?' Greenberg
Princeton, NJ; Princeton University Press, 1996

A Study of Hospital Waiting Lists in Cardiff, 1953–1954
Fred Grundy
Cardiff: United Cardiff Hospitals, 1956

Philippe Halsman's Jump Book
Philippe Halsman
Andre Deutsch, 1959
'This book shows 178

jumps executed by some of the most prominent and important people of our society.' The subjects of Halsman's photographic portraits include Salvador Dali, Richard Nixon, and Edith Sitwell, who described him as 'a horrid little man', a view shared by the photographer Cecil Beaton, who commented, 'A more undignified, ugly collection than his "Jumpers" cannot be imagined.'

The Problem of Nonsense Linguistics
Goran Hammarstrom
Stockholm: Almqvist and Wiksell, 1971

The Romance of Rayon
Arnold Henry Hard
Manchester: Whittaker and Robinson, 1933

Anglo-Saxon Writs
Florence Elizabeth Harmer
Manchester: Manchester University Press, 1952

Short-term Visual Information Forgetting
A. H. C. Van Der Heijden
International Library of Psychology and Routledge, 1981

What to Say When You Talk to Yourself
Shad Helmstetter
Scottsdale, Ariz.: Grindle Press, 1982

Locomotive Boiler Explosions
Christian H. Hewison
Newton Abbot: David and Charles, 1983
'Always engrossing… sometimes disturbing.'
(Book club advertisement)

The Madam as Entrepreneur: Career Management in House Prostitution
Barbara Sherman Heyl
New Brunswick, NJ: Transaction Books, 1979

New Corpus of Anglo-
Saxon Great Square-
Headed Brooches
John Hines
Boydell and Brewer, 1997

Your Answer to Invasion –
Ju-Jitsu
James Hipkiss
F. W. Bridges, 1941

The Dot in Semitic
Palaeography
Harting Hirschfield
*Philadelphia, Pa.:
Jewish Quarterly Review,
1919*

The Toothbrush: its Use
and Abuse
Isador Hirschfield
*New York: Dental Items of
Interest Publishing Co., 1939*

Peking Pigeons and
Pigeon-Flutes
Harned Pettus Hoose
*Peking: College of Chinese
Studies, California College in
China, 1938*

Red-White-Black as a
Mode of Thought. A Study
of Triadic Classification by
Colours in the Ritual
Symbolism and Cognitive
Thought of the Peoples of
the Lower Congo
A. Jacobson-Widing
*Stockholm: Almqvist and
Wiksell, 1979*

Bogs of the Northeast
Charles W. Johnson
*Hanover, NH: University
Press of New England, 1985*

Teach Yourself Air
Navigation
"Kaspar"
*The English Universities
Press, 1942*

How to Fire an Employee
Daniel T. Kingsley
Bicester: Facts on File, 1984

Oh Angry Sea (a-ab-ba
hu-luh-ha): the History
of a Sumerian
Congregational Lament
Raphael Kutscher
*New Haven, Conn.: Yale
University Press, 1975*

Fish-Hooks in Africa and their Distribution
Sture Lagercrantz
Stockholm: Statens Etnografiska Museum, 1934
Lagercrantz later turned his attention to:
Penis Sheaths and their Distribution in Africa
Uppsala: Uppsala University, 1976

The Railways of Tottenham
G. H. Lake
Greenlake Publications, 1945

The Trombone in the Middle Ages and the Renaissance
George B. Lane
Bloomington, Ind.: Indiana University Press, 1982

The 'Walking Stick' Method of Self-Defence
Herbert Gordon Lang
Athletic Publications, 1926
A manual illustrating numerous ways of whacking someone with a stick. It contains chapters with such evocative titles as 'Flicks' and 'Flips', 'Cuts' and 'Active Stick Play'.

BERTHOLD LAUFER

Berthold Laufer (1874-1934) of Chicago deserves special mention as the distinguished author of a veritable library of over 100 fascinating works. They were mostly published in Leiden by E. J. Brill or in Chicago by the Field Museum of Natural History, and include, in chronological order of publication:

1899
Petroglyphs on the Amoor

1906
The Bird Chariot

1912
Confucius and his Portraits
The Discovery of a Lost Book

History of the Finger-
print System

1913
The Application of the
Tibetan Sexagenary
Cycle
Arabic and Chinese Trade
in Walrus and Narwhal
Ivory

1914
Was Oderic of Pordenone
Ever in Tibet?
The Sexagenary Cycle
Once More
Three Tokhavian
Bagatelles
Bird Divination Among
the Tibetans

1915
The Eskimo Screw as a
Culture-Historical
Problem
Asbestos and Salamander

1916
Cardan's Suspension in
China

1917
The Reindeer and its
Domestication
Loan-Words in Tibetan

1923
Use of Human Skulls and
Bones in Tibet
Oriental Theatricals

1925
Chinese Baskets

1926
Ostrich Egg-shell Cups of
Mesopotamia and the
Ostrich in Ancient and
Modern Times

1927
Insect Musicians and
Cricket Champions of
China
Agate (section on
archaeology and folklore
by Laufer)

1928
The Giraffe in History and
Art

c.1930
**Felt: How It Was Made
and Used in Ancient
Times**
Geophagy (earth-eating)

1931
**The Domestication of the
Cormorant in China and
Japan**

1938 (Posthumous)
American Plant Migration

Historic Bubbles
Frederic Leake
Suckling and Galloway, 1896

**The One-Leg Resting
Position (Nilotenstellung)
in Africa and Elsewhere**
Gerhard Lindblom
*Stockholm: Statens
Ethnografiska Museum, 1949*
A survey of cultures in
which people stand on one
leg, with photographs and a
map of where people who
do so live.

**Benedictine Maledictions:
Liturgical Cursing in
Romanesque France**
Lester K. Little
*Ithaca, NY: Cornell
University Press, 1993*

**Aeroplane Designing for
Amateurs**
Victor Lougheed
n.p., 1912

**Bead Making in
Scandinavia in the Early
Middle Ages**
Agneta Lundström
*Stockholm: Almqvist and
Wiksell, 1976*

A Toddler's Guide to the Rubber Industry
D. Lowe
Leicester: De Montfort Press, 1947
A reissue in book form of essays published in the *India-Rubber Review* employing an 'Alice in Rubberland' framework. As the *India-Rubber Journal* said of Mr Lowe's other book, *A Toddler's Guide to Big Business*, 'The book is written in satirical vein, but it points a moral and in parts makes amusing reading.'

Androgynous Objects: String Bags in Central New Guinea
Maureen Anne MacKenzie
Philadelphia, Pa.: Harwood Academic Publishers, 1992

How to Fill Mental Cavities
Bill Maltz
Beverly Hills, Ca.: Marlbro, 1978

List of Persons Whose Names Have Changed in Massachusetts, 1780–1892
Massachusetts, Secretary of the Commonwealth
Baltimore, Md.: Genealogical Publishing Co., 1972

Wall-to-Wall America: A Cultural History of Post-Office Murals in the Great Depression
Karal Ann Marling
Minneapolis, Minn.: University of Minnesota Press, 1982

A User's Guide to Capitalism and Schizophrenia
Brian Massumi
Cambridge, Mass.: MIT Press, 1992

Fifty New Creative Poodle Grooming Styles
Faye Meadows
New York: Arco Publishing Co., 1981

Oedipus in the Trobriands
E. Spiro Melford
*Chicago, Ill.: University of
Chicago Press, 1982*

Manhole Covers of Los Angeles
Robert and Mimi Melnick
*Los Angeles, Ca.: Dawson's
Book Shop, 1974*

A Do-It-Yourself Submachine Gun
Gerard Metral
*Boulder, Col.: Paladin Press,
1995*

The Crumhorn: Its History, Design, Repertory and Technique
Kenton Terry Meyer
*Ann Arbor, Mich.: UMI
Research, 1983*

Correct Mispronunciations of Some South Carolina Names
Claude and Irene Neuffer
*Columbia, SC: University of
South Carolina Press, 1984*

Great Abstruse Authors
Frank Noah
*Chicago, Ill.: Christopher
Publishing House, 1927*
Noah seeks to prove that
Shakespeare, Tennyson,
Churchill, Barrie, and
Kipling are all pseudonyms
'devised by a secret method'.

The Impact of Global Warming on Texas
Gerald R. North, Jurgen
Schmandt, and Judith
Clarkson
*Austin, Tx.: University of
Texas Press, 1995*

Nuclear War: What's In It For You?
Ground Zero War
Foundation
New York: Pocket Books, 1982

Child-spacing in Tropical Africa
Hilary J. Page and Ron
Lesthaege (eds.)
Academic Press, 1981

LEADERSHIP SECRETS OF ATTILA THE HUN

WESS ROBERTS PhD

'An imaginative and colourful approach to relating leadership principles that have long served those having the will to lead.'
Ken Blanchard, PhD, co-author of *The One Minute Manager*

A History of Orgies
Burgo Partridge
Anthony Blond, 1958

Defensive Tactics with Flashlights
John G. Peters Jr.
Northbrook, Ill.: Calibre Press, 1983

Little-Known Sisters of Well-Known Men
Sarah G. Pomeroy
Boston, Mass.: Dana Estes, 1912

The History and Romance of Elastic Webbing Since the Dawn of Time
Clifford A. Richmond
Easthampton, Mass.: The Author, n.d.

Leadership Secrets of Attila the Hun
Wess Roberts
New York: Bantam Books, 1989

Helium in Canada from 1926 to 1931
P. V. Rosewarne
Ottawa: F. A. Acland, 1931
Helium followed egg-laying (see page 51) as Canada's principal preoccupation.

How to Write While You Sleep
Elizabeth Irvin Ross
Cincinnati, Ohio: Writer's Digest Books, 1985

The Androgynous Manager
Alice Sargent
New York: Amacom, 1980

A History of Victorian Skirt Grips
Mary Sawdon
Cambridge: Midsummer Books, 1995

Movie Stars in Bathtubs
Jack Scagnetti
Middle Village, NY: Jonathan David Publishers, 1975

Violence as Communication
Alex Schmid and Janny De Graaf
Beverly Hills, Ca.: Sage Publications, 1982

Ships' Bilge Pumps: A History of Their Development, 1500–1900
Thomas J, Oeterling
Chatham Publishing, 1997

British Goblins
William Wirt Sikes
n.p., 1879

Cannibalism and the Common Law: A Victorian Yachting Tragedy
Alfred William Brian Simpson

Chicago, Ill.: University of Chicago Press, 1984

Hours and Earnings in the Leather-glove Industry
Rebecca Glover Smaltz
Washington, DC: United States Government Printing Office, 1934

From the Monotremes to the Madonna. A Study of the Breast in Culture and Religion
Fabius Zachary Snoop
John Bale, Sons and Danielson, 1928
'The poet... takes the universe to be only an overwhelming maternity... perfecting the breast was Nature's supreme endeavour', as can be assessed in such chapters as:
    The Fragrant Bosom of
        Aphrodite
    The Bosom of the
        Father
    Aaron's Breastplate
    Mountains of Myrrh
    The Bloody Teat
    Vests

**Chinese Bondage in Peru:
A History of the Chinese
Coolie in Peru, 1849–1874**
W. Stewart
*Durham, NC: Duke
University Press, 1951*

Hawaiian Fishponds
Catherine Summers
*Honolulu: Bishop's Museum
Press, 1964*

**Selling Mother's Milk:
The Wetnurse Business in
France, 1715-1914**
George D. Sussman
*Urbana, Ill.: University of
Illinois Press, 1982*

**Paleopathological and
Paleoepidemiological
Study of Osseous Syphilis
in the Skulls of the Edo
Period**
Takao Suzuki
*Tokyo: University of Tokyo
Press, 1984*

How to Avoid Huge Ships
John W. Trimmer
*Centreville, Md.: Cornell
Maritime Press, 1993*

**Improvement of the Steady
Floating Random Walk
Monte Carlo Method Near
Straight Line and Circular
Boundaries, with
Application to
Groundwater Flow**
James Harold Turner
*Manhattan, Ka.: Kansas
Water Resources Research
Institute, 1977*

**Holding the Line: The
Telephone in Old Order
Mennonite and Amish
Life**
Diane Zimmerman Umble
*Baltimore, Md.: Johns
Hopkins University Press,
1996*

**Umbrellas and parts of
umbrellas (except handles).
Report to the President on
Investigation no. TEA-I-6
under Section 301(b)(1) of
the Trade Expansion Act of
1962**
*Washington, DC: US Tariff
Commission, 1964*

Standardizing the Hospitallier Brothers of Saint John of God Library... A nonpareil vade mecum with causative prolegomenary analysis and synthesis of the master Lynn-Peterson classification, 2nd ed, based on the Radio studiorum prescribed by the Sacred Congregation of Rites for seminary and university studies and the standardized selective bibliography of the OSJD Library in Los Angeles and with resultant OSJD manuals
Mary Carol Theresa Wagner
Washington, DC: n.p., 1967

Careers in Dope
Dan Waldorf
Englewood Cliffs, NJ: Prentice-Hall, 1973

The Famines of the World
Cornelius Walford
Edward Stanford, 1879
An exhaustive listing, starting in 1708 BC.

The Infancy and Development of Linoleum Floorcloth
Frederick Walton
Simpkin, Marshall, Hamilton, Kent, 1925
By the inventor of linoleum, high quality 'Lincrusta Walton' – a type of embossed lino used for dados and panelling, not to be confused with High Quality Wilton – and flexible metallic tubing. He died, at the age of 94, in 1928 leaving £54,116 gross, £53,633 nett.

The Darjeeling Disaster – Its Bright Side
F. W. Warne
Calcutta: The Methodist Publishing House, 1900

Nasology; or, Hints Towards a Classification of Noses
Eden Warwick (pseudonym of George Jabet)
A. Bentley, 1848

Busted Tractors and Rusty Knuckles: Norwegian Torque Wrench Techniques and Other Fine Points of Tractor Restoration
Roger L. Welsch
Osceola, Wis.: Motorbooks International, 1997

Music in the Typewriting Room
H. E. White
Sir Isaac Pitman, 1947
The use of strict-tempo music to get the typing pool to increase its output.

Clinical Hat Pegs for Students and Graduates
R. J. Willan
Heinemann, 1951

California Drawbridges
Bernard C. Winn
San Francisco, Ca.: Incline Press, 1995

Julius Caesar and His Public Image
Zvi Yavetz
Ithaca, NY: Cornell University Press, 1982

The Influence of Mountains upon the Development of Human Intelligence
Geoffrey Winthrop Young
Glasgow: Jackson, Son and Co. and Glasgow University Press, 1957

Lappish Bear Graves in Northern Sweden
Inge Zachrisson and Elizabeth Iregren
Stockholm: Almqvist and Wiksell, 1974

BAD HAIR DAY

A selective bibliography of pogonology and trichology:

Philosophy of Red Hair
Anon.
J. Bales and Sons, 1890

The Unconscious Significance of Hair
George Charles Berg
George Allen and Unwin, 1951

Pro Sacerdotum Barbis
Giovanni Pierio Valeriano Bolzani
Rome: n.p., 1531
Argues the case for priests wearing beards.

The Classification of Mankind by the Hair and Wool of Their Heads, with an Answer to Dr Prichard's Assertion, that 'The Covering of the Head of the Negro Is Hair, Properly So Termed, and Not Wool'
Peter Arrell Browne
Philadelphia, Pa.: n.p., 1850

Rhythmical Essays on the Beard Question
W. Carter
n.p., 1868

Construction of an Ancient Egyptian Wig in the British Museum
James Stevens Cox
St Peter Port: Toucan Press, 1994
Cox introduced the permanent wave into England. He was also the author of:
Fortune-telling by the Disposition of Moles
St Peter Port: Toucan Press, 1969

Pogonologia; or, A Philosophical and Historical Essay on Beards
Jacques Antoine Dulaure
Exeter: Printed by R. Thorn, sold by T. Cadell, 1786
'A man without a beard would be much less surprising now-a-days, than a bearded woman, which proves how unnatural our tastes and customs are.'

How to Shave Yourself
'An Expert'
Van and Alexander, 1906

The Inheritance of Hairy Ear Rims
Reginald Ruggles Gates and P. N. Bhaduri
Edinburgh: Mankind Quarterly, 1961

The Philosophy of Beards
Thomas S. Gowing
Ipswich: J. Haddock, c.1850

The Loathsomenesse of Long Haire… with the Concurrent Judgement of Divines both Old and New Against It. With an Appendix Against Painting, Spots, Naked Breasts, etc
Rev. Thomas Hall
J. G. for N. Webb and W. Grantham, 1654

Beard Shaving, and the Common Use of the Razor, an Unnatural, Irrational, Unmanly, Ungodly and Fatal Fashion Among Christians
William Henry Henslowe
W. E. Painter, 1847

The Direction of Hair in Animals and Man
Walter Kidd
Adam and Charles Black, 1903

Grow Your Own Hair
Ron Maclaren
Glasgow: Healthway Publications, 1947

The Mysteries, Secrets and Whole Art of an Easy Shave
Joseph Morton
L. U. Gill, 1893

Ancient and Modern Beards
G. Price
n.p., 1893

The Unlovelinesse of Love-Locks
William Prynne
n.p., 1628

Some Account of the Beard and the Moustachio
John Adey Repton
J. B. Nichols, 1839

New Views on Baldness
Henry Paul Truefitt
n.p., 1863

Barbalogia
Giuseppe Valeriano de Vannetti
Roveredo: n.p., 1759
Goes into the problem of whether Adam was born with a beard or not, coming down in favour of those who hold that 'The father of the human race had a beard from the first instant of his life. All men, before the Flood, had one too.'

The Folly and Evil of Shaving
'Xerxes'
n.p., 1854

FACTS AT YOUR FINGERTIPS

Dictionaries, encyclopaedias, and reference books no home should be without:

Bibliography of Mangrove Research, 1600–1975
Anon.
Paris: UNESCO, 1981

The Great Encyclopedia of Universal Knowledge
Anon.
Odhams, 1933
A small octavo book.

How To Do It; or, Directions for Knowing or Doing Everything Needful
Anon.
New York: J. F. Tingley, 1864

An Illustrated Inventory of Famous Dismembered Works of Art
Anon.
Paris: UNESCO, 1974

**Liver Building, Liverpool.
List of Stop Cocks**
Anon.
*Toxteth: J. Litchfield,
Printer, 1912*
Here is the long-lost record of the complex plumbing arrangements of the Liver Building. Only here can be discovered the fact that stop cock No. 2 on the tenth floor, bottom tank, south side, shuts off the gentlemen's lavatories and bar, and that the cisterns in the National Health Section

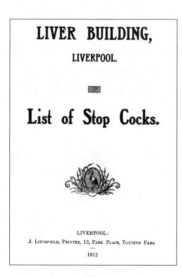

Offices on the ground floor can be found on iron girders behind the lifts one floor up.

**Rubbing Along in
Burmese**
Anon.
*Simla: Directorate of Welfare
and Education, Adjutant
General's Branch GHQ, 1944*

**Early Victorian Water
Engineers**
Geoffrey Morse Binnie
Thomas Telford, 1981

**The Penis Inserts of
Southeast Asia: An
Annotated Bibliography
with an Overview and
Comparative Perspectives**
Donald E. Brown, James W. Edwards, and Ruth Moore
*Berkeley, Ca.: Center for
South and Southeast Asia
Studies, 1988*
Listed by one bookseller as a 'self-help' title.

A Register of Royal and Baronial Domestic Minstrels, 1272-1327
Constance Bullock-Davies
Boydell, 1986

The New Guide of the Conversation in Portuguese and English in Two Parts
Pedro Carolino
Peking 'And to the house of all the booksellers of Paris', 1869 (2nd edition)
This phrase book reaches a level of brilliance quite unsurpassed by any other. Portuguese-English conversations are intelligently constructed by the author, whose tools were French-English and French-Portuguese dictionaries. The result squares the triangle of language uniquely and effectively:

Dialogue 43: The french language
Do you study?
Yes, sir, I attempts to translate of french by portuguese.
Then you learn the french language?
You do well the french language becomes us all days too much necessary.
What books have you there?
It is a grammar and a vocabulary.
Do you know already the principal grammars rules?
I am appleed my self at to learn its by heart.
What work do you translate thither?
It is a collection choice pieces in prose.
Don't you read yet the poets?
The poems are yet too difficult by me.
Do you compose without doubt also some small discourses in french?
Not yet I don't make that some exercises
Do you speak french alwais?
Some times; though I flay it yet.
You jest, you does express you self very well.

Jews at a Glance
Mac Davis
New York: Hebrew Publishing Co., 1956
From Abraham to Adolph Zukor, 'pioneer with a magic lantern'.

The Irish Word Processing Guide
Dolores Donovan and Diarmuid Herlihy (eds.)
Dublin: Hamilton Press, 1981

Six Language Dictionary of Plastics and Rubber Technology
A. F. Dorian
Iliffe, 1965

The Encyclopedia of Medical Ignorance
Ronald Duncan and M. Weston-Smith (eds.)
Oxford: Pergamon Press, 1984

Encyclopedia of Pocket Knives
Roy Ehrhardt
Kansas City, Mo.: Heart of America Press, (3 vols.), n.d.

A Compendium of the Biographical Literature on Deceased Entomologists
Pamela Gilbert
British Museum (Natural History), 1977

Irish Swordsmen of France
Richard Francis Hayes
Dublin: M. H. Gill and Son, 1934
Hayes was also the author of:
Biographical Dictionary of Irishmen in France
Dublin: M. H. Gill and Son, 1949

Sea Terms and Phrases: English-Spanish: Spanish-English
Graham Hewlett
Charles Griffin, 1907

Abbott's Encyclopedia of Rope Tricks
Stewart James
Colon, Mich.: Abbott's Magic Novelty Co., 1945

**Messing Records,
1272–1803**
Oswald Greenwaye Knapp
Society of Genealogists, 1937
Knapp went on to compile:
**The Parish Registers of
Piddlehinton, Co. Dorset,
1539–1652**
Society of Genealogists, 1938

**A Catalogue of Swedish
Local Postage Stamps,
issued from 1941 to 1947**
Raymond George Lister
Dumfries: K. Jahr, 1952

**An Annotated
Bibliography of
Evaporation**
Grace J. Livingston
Washington, DC: n.p., 1909

**Five Hundred Questions
on Subjects Requiring
Investigation in the Social
Condition of Natives of
India**
Rev. J. Long
*Calcutta: Baptist Mission
Press, 1862*
Questions answered
include:

Are dwarfs numerous?
Spitting, why practiced
  so much by Hindus?
What are the recreations of
  females – is kite flying
  such?
In what respect are boatmen
  equal to sailors?

**Prominent People of New
Brunswick**
Charles Herbert MacLean
*Saint John, NB: The
Biographical Society of
Canada, 1937*

**Who's Who in Cocker
Spaniels**
Marion Frances Robinson
Mangrum
Norman, Okla.: n.p., 1944

**Lights! Catalogue of
Worldwide Matchbox
Labels with the Word
'Light' in the Title**
Raymond W. Norris
*Royston: British Matchbox
Label and Booklet Society,
1983*

Railway Literature, 1556–1830
Robert Alexander Peddie
Grafton and Co., 1931
Covers the interesting period in railway history before trains were invented.

The Encyclopedia of Alcoholism
Robert O'Brien and Morris Chafetz
Bicester: Facts on File, 1983

Biographical Dictionary of Wax Modellers
Edward Pyke
Oxford: Oxford University Press, (Vol. 1), 1973; The Author, (Vols 2 and 3), 1983

Prostitutes of Hyderabad
M. Rangarao
Hyderabad: Hyderabad Association for Moral and Social Hygiene, 1970

A Dictionary of International Slurs
A. A. Roback
Cambridge, Mass.: Sci–Art Publishers, 1944

Manuale di Conversazione: Italiano-Groenlandese
Ciro Sozio and Mario Fantin
Bologna: Tamari Editori, 1962

How to Abandon Ship
Philip Richards and John J. Banigan
New York: Cornell Maritime Press, 1942 (2nd edition)

'NOW with 40 more pages of NEW material'. In a useful pocket size so that it can be carried by every man or woman about to ship out.

The Proverbs of British Guiana
Rev. James Speirs
Demerara: The Argosy Co., 1902
'No. 539: Luck mo' better dan han'some.
No. 772: Rum Done, Fun Done.'

Selective Bibliography of the Literature of Lubrication
Nathan Van Patten and Grace S. Lewis
Kingston, Ont.: N. Van Patten, 1926

1001 Things You Can Get Free
Mort Weisinger
New York: Bantam, 1957
'A Fabulous New Treasury of America's Choisest Giveaway Items.'
'Ever envy the way the heroes in Hollywood films achieve that well-groomed look by the perfect way they knot their tie? It's easy to obtain the same effect, if you know how. For an illustrated brochure on how to tie a better knot, send for "Tie Lore Booklet"...'
'Free movie to show in your own home: "Lifeline". Action picture which stars famous actor Thomas Mitchell and tells the exciting story of rope and twine.'

The Illustrated Encyclopedia of Metal Lunch Boxes
Allen Woodall and Sean Brickell
Atglen, Pa.: Schiffer Publications, 1997

6

MARVELS OF SCIENCE

Boffins' brilliant books

Petroleum in Leather
Anon.
Rochester, NY: Vacuum Oil Co., 1896
On curing leather; with an initial instruction to readers that all earlier editions should be thrown away.

The Coming Disaster Worse Than the H-bomb, Astronomically, Geologically and Scientifically Proven. The Coal Beds, Ice Ages, Tides, and Coming Soon, a Great Wave and Flood Caused by a Shift of the Axis of the Earth From the Gyroscopic Action of Our Solar System. Why Our Solar System Works.
Adam D. Barber
Washington, DC: Barber Scientific Foundation, 1954
Barber's theory is that the Earth shifts on its axis every 9,000 years, taking a mere ninety minutes to do so. The last occasion resulted in Noah's Flood; the next is imminent…

The Biochemist's Songbook
Harold Baum
Oxford: Pergamon Press, 1982
This successful, albeit improbable combination, has been followed by Baum's *Biorhythms* (Learn Through Music, 1984) in which O-Level biology is set to words and music.

Atomic Bombing: How to Protect Yourself

Watson Davis

New York: William H. Wise and Co., 1950

'Radioactivity is like a dog shaking itself after being in the water.'

'Steaks are a must in the diet of the burn patient.'

'American skyscrapers... are built on heavy steel frames. Buildings such as these... would withstand the blast of an atomic bomb.'

'Curl up in a ball as you hit the ground.'

Water, Not Convex: The Earth Not a Globe!

William Carpenter
The Author, 1871
Carpenter was a British
follower of 'Parallax'
(see page 76) and later
emigrated to America to
promote his Flat Earth
Theory; there he wrote:

One Hundred Proofs that the Earth is Not a Globe

Baltimore, Md.: The Author, 1885

Water Wave Propagation over Uneven Bottoms

Maarten W. Dingemans
River Edge, NJ: World Scientific Publishing Co., 1997

Romping Through Physics

Otto Willi Gail
G. Routledge and Sons, 1933

What's Wanted. A List of 895 Needed Inventions

Institute of Patentees
Institute of Patentees, 3rd edition, 1933
A useful source of ideas for
the budding inventor:
lipstick-proof linen; a
bullet-proof stroboscope; an
automatic refrigerator for
under £3.10s.0d.; a machine
for the dining table to pick
winkles from their shells;
improvements in deckchairs
whereby the user can sit
sideways; a slot-machine for
use at post offices to give
two halfpennies for a penny;
and, perhaps most useful of
all, a domestic machine for
use in private houses for
getting rid of books by
pulping.

How to Draw a Straight Line

Sir Alfred Bray Kempe
Macmillan, 1877
'The Unexplored Fields are
still vast.'

The Human Gyroscope: A Consideration of the Gyroscopic Rotation of the Earth as Mechanism of the Evolution of Terrestrial Living Forms. Explaining the Phenomenon of Sex:

**Its Origin and
Development and Its
Significance in the
Evolutionary Process**
Arabella Kenealy
Hudson and Keans, 1934

**Flights of Fancy: Early
Aviation in Battersea and
Wandsworth**
Patrick Loobey
*Recreation Department,
Wandsworth Borough
Council, 1981*
Revealing the astonishing
information that the Wright
Brothers were busy building
aeroplanes in Battersea,
South London, in the early
1900s. However, these were
not *the* Wright Brothers,
Wilbur and Orville, but two
other Wright Brothers,
Howard and Warwick,
manufacturers of bespoke
aircraft, including, in 1907,
a helicopter for Frederico
Capone of Naples. Tested
on Norbury golf links, it
achieved a maximum
altitude of two feet.

**Light and Truth, M's
Invention for Destroying
All Foul Air and Fire
Damp in Coal Pits
(Proving Also) the
Scriptures to be Right
which Learned Men are
Mystifying, and Proving
the Orang Outang or
Monkey the Most Unlikely
Thing Under the Sun to be
the Serpent That Beguiled
Our First Parents**
William Martin
Newcastle: The Author, 1838
William Martin
(1782–1838), the eccentric
author of numerous esoteric
pamphlets, was the brother
of John Martin, the painter
of apocalyptic scenes, and
Jonathan Martin, who
set fire to York Minster
in 1829.

Zetetic Astronomy
'Parallax' (pseudonym of
Samuel Birley Rowbotham)
*Birmingham: W. Cornish,
1849*
In a series of experiments
conducted along the

'Bedford Level' in Cambridgeshire in 1838, 'Parallax' attempted to demonstrate that he could see distant objects sited on the canal and that cannon balls fired vertically fell straight down, thus proving that the Earth is flat and non-rotating. His findings were published in this remarkable work, the title of which derives from the Greek, meaning 'I discover for myself'. He had many zetetic followers, including William Carpenter (see page 76), Lady Elizabeth Anne Mould Blount, John Hampden, William Edgell (see page 79) and others who wrote books along similar lines, starting a 'Flat Earth' cult that continues to this day.

The Romance of Holes in Bread. A Plea for the Recognition of the Scientific Laboratory as the Testing Place for Truth
I. K. Russell

Easton, Pa.: The Chemical Publishing Co., 1924

A New General Theory of the Teeth of Wheels
Edward Sang
A. and C. Black, 1852
Sang was Professor of Mechanical Philosophy in the Imperial School, Muhendis-Hana Berrii, Constantinople.

Chemistrianity (Popular Knowledge of Chemistry). A Poem; Also an Oratorical Verse on each known Chemical Element in the Universe, Giving Description, Properties, Sources, Preparation and Chief Uses
John Carrington Sellars
Birkenhead: The Author, c.1873

Seven Years of 'Manifold': 1968–1980
Ian Stewart and John Jaworski (eds.)
Nantwich: Shiva Publishing, c.1981

Articles on mathematical problems – including, perhaps, how 1980 minus 1968 equals seven?

The Diseases of Electrical Machinery
George Wilfred Stubbings
E. and F. N. Spon, 1939

Does the Earth Rotate?
William Westfield (pseudo-nym of William Edgell)
*Radstock; n.p., 1914
(republished Bath: F. Goodall, 1927)*
Westfield was also the author of:
Is the Earth a Fixture? Yes! And the Sun Travels
n.p., 1915

A Study of Splashes
Arthur Mason Worthington
Longmans, Green, 1908
A Study of Splashes describes with near-obsessive attention to detail the astonishing spectacle of a 'water drop weighing 0.4 grams falling 137 cm (4½ feet) into milk mixed with water'.

Optimistically aiming it at 'the general reader', Arthur Worthington explains how his *magnum opus* grew out of his 1894 Royal Institution lecture, 'The Splash of a Drop', which was reprinted in the *Romance of Science* series, published – perhaps surprisingly – by the Society for the Promotion of Christian Knowledge. This extraordinary book contains no fewer than 197 photographs, all of which are virtually identical.

Flow of Water Through Six-inch Pipe Bends
David L. Yarnell
Washington, DC: United States Department of Agriculture, 1937

7

DIRTY BOOKS

Books on manure – and worse

Bodily Functions: Stories, Poems, and a Letter on the Subject of Bowel Movement Addressed to Sam J. Lundwall on the Occasion of his Birthday February 24th, A.D. 1991
Brian W. Aldiss
Avernus, 1991

An Essay Upon Wind; with Curious Anecdotes of Eminent Peteurs. Humbly Dedicated to the Lord Chancellor
Anon. (alleged to be Charles James Fox)
'Printed and sold by all the Booksellers in Town and Country', 1787
'I take it there are five or six different species of Farts, and which are perfectly distinct from each other, both in weight, and smell.

First, the sonorous, and
    full-toned Fart;
Second, the double Fart;
Third, the soft-fizzing
    Fart;
Fourth, the wet Fart;
and Fifth, the sullen,
    wind bound Fart.'

'Fart No.4 – Commonly called the wet Fart, is very easily procured. Let any person fond of overeating, cram himself with pies, custards, whip-syllabub, prunes, &c. &c. and he will do his business with effec-tual dispatch, so as to need an immediate washing. Ladies produce this species of Fart better than gentlemen, so that it is adviseable to try this experiment upon a strong, healthy young lady of about eighteen, and who is apt to be hungry,'

The 'Afterthoughts upon Farting shewing its great utility; with curious Anecdotes of Eminent Farters' gives warning of overindulgence in the art by quoting the case of Simon Tup, 'the Farting Blacksmith' from Kirkeaton, Yorkshire, who: '… had the singular and ingenious talent of accompanying any instrument… which he could perform so admirably in time, tone and tune, as to deceive the nicest judges… The fate of this poor fellow was very melancholy; by an uncommon exertion which he made in the famous song 'Blow high, blow low', he unfortunately broke a blood-vessel of which he instantly died.'

Pooh! Pooh! Pooh! Pooh! A Poem By One of Job's Comforters
Anon.
n.p., 1839

Stray Leaves from Japanese Papers
Anon.
Bourne, Johnson and Latimer, c.1870
The ultimate lavatory book. Approximately 400 blank leaves of 'Japanese sanitary paper. Antiseptic. Hygienic. A perfectly pure article for the Toilet and Lavatory, and a preventative for piles… as soft as silk and although it is very tough, will readily dissolve in water… confidently recommended as the best article ever produced for the particular purpose for which it is intended.'
Also, from the same publishers, but in paper covers rather than maroon cloth, *Nothing but Leaves*.

JAPANESE
SANITARY PAPER

ANTISEPTIC. HYGIENIC.

A perfectly pure article for the Toilet and Lavatory, and a preventive of piles.

This most useful Household Requisite is made of the very best materials, entirely free from such pernicious chemicals as Sulphuric Acid, Lime, Potash, &c., which are used so extensively in the bleaching of paper.

The Japanese Sanitary Paper is almost as soft as silk, and although it is very tough, will readily dissolve in water.

This paper is confidently recommended as the best article ever produced for the particular purpose for which it is intended.

As a SANITARY PAPER it is free from all poisonous chemicals, and as a CURL PAPER it is soft, and yet so strong as to bear a tight twist.

Price 1s. per Packet.

Uniform with the above, but in Paper Covers.

"NOTHING BUT LEAVES."

Price 6d. each.

The Water of Life. A Treatise on Urine-therapy
John W. Armstrong
True Health Publishing Co., 1949
The Indian edition is euphemistically listed in *Indian Books in Print* as 'Wine therapy'.

Wind Breaks: Coming to Terms with Flatulence
Terry Dorcen Bolin and Rosemary Stanton
New York: Bantam Books, 1995

Arresting Disclosures. A Report on the Strange Findings in Undergarments Washed with Soap and Water, and Popularly Supposed to be Clean, Fresh and Wholesome
John A. Bolton
Leicester: J. and J. H. Vice, 1924
A copy of this book has been seen in a bookseller's catalogue described as good, 'but not spotless'.

Trickle Treat: Diaperless Infant Toilet Training
Laurie Boucke
Montrose, Ca.: White and Boucke Publishers, 1991

The Urine Dance of the Zuni Indians of New Mexico
Captain John G. Bourke
Ann Arbor, Mich.: American Association for the Advancement of Science, 1885

Arresting Disclosures.

By JOHN A. BOLTON, M.I.H. F.R.G.S.

A REPORT ON THE STRANGE FINDINGS IN UNDER-
GARMENTS WASHED WITH SOAP AND WATER,
AND POPULARLY SUPPOSED TO BE CLEAN, FRESH
AND WHOLESOME.

Illustrated by over one hundred and thirty Micro-photographs.

Price 2/6

Gratis to "Chilprufe" wearers.

In this brief account John Bourke, a captain in the US Army Third Cavalry, describes how on 17 November 1881 he was taken as a guest to witness a singular ritual known as the 'urine dance'. Twelve Zuni Indian dancers, some wearing cotton nightcaps and one, appropriately, in an india-rubber coat, entered and sang an obscene ditty: 'their song was apparently a ludicrous reference to everything and everybody in sight'. An *olla* (a kind of cooking pot) containing urine was brought in ceremoniously, 'of which the filthy brutes drank heartily'. This appetizer was followed by a tin pail containing over two gallons of urine, which the performers guzzled with apparent relish.

Captain Bourke was assured that on other occasions the rite was extended to the consumption of excrement, but this was too much for him, and without waiting to test the truth of this claim, he made an excuse and left.

A Sanitary Crusade through the East and Australia
Robert Boyle
Glasgow: Boyle, 1892

Survey of Toilet Facilities for the Public in Chain Stores, Cooperative Retail Stores and Department Stores
Stoke-on-Trent: British Ceramic Sanitaryware Manufacturers, 1965

The Gas We Pass: The Story of Farts
Shinta Cho
Brooklyn, NY: Kane/Miller Book Publishers, 1994

Smut: An Anatomy of Dirt
Christian Engensberger
New York: Seabury, 1972

**The Muck Manual: A
Practical Treatise on the
Nature and Values of
Manures**
F. Falkner
John Murray, 1843

**Dirt: A Social History as
Seen Through the Uses
and Abuses of Dirt**
Terence McLaughlin
*New York: Stein and Day,
1971*

The Sewage Question
Frederick Charles Krepp
Longmans Green, 1867
What's the answer?

**The Golden Fountain:
Complete Guide to Urine
Therapy**
Coen van der Kroon
*Banbury: Amethyst Books,
1996*

**The Law Relating to
Sewers and Drains**
Alexander Macmorran and
W. Addington Willis
Butterworth, 1904

**How to Test Your Urine at
Home**
B. C. Meyrowitz
*Girard, Ka.: Haldeman-Julius,
c.1935*

**The Time Registering
Closet. A New System
Whereby Much Valuable
Time of Employees is Saved**
Monitor Closet Company
(Promotional booklet)
*Monitor Closet Co., Warehouse
Point, Conn.: 1892*
'In these times of close
competition and small
profits it behoves the
employer to get the best
possible results from the
labor of those in his employ
in a legitimate way and at the
same time study the comfort
of the employee... Overseers
of manufactories fully realize
that much valuable time is
"fooled" away by operatives
absenting themselves from
their places at frequent and
unnecessarily long intervals
to visit the Water Closet, and
often a number are out at the
same time, thus losing many

MANUFACTURERS' ATTENTION

—— IS CALLED TO THE——

TIME REGISTERING CLOSET.

A NEW SYSTEM

Whereby Much Valuable Time of Employees is Saved.

LOOK. READ. INVESTIGATE.

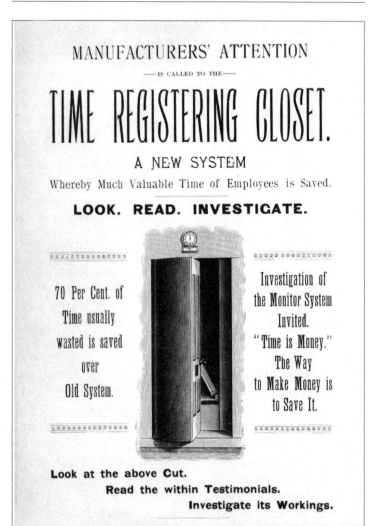

70 Per Cent. of
Time usually
wasted is saved
over
Old System.

Investigation of
the Monitor System
Invited.
"Time is Money."
The Way
to Make Money is
to Save It.

Look at the above Cut.
Read the within Testimonials.
Investigate its Workings.

Patented in the United States, Great Britain and Canada. United States Patents
granted April 8th, 1890, and June 9th, 1891. Other patents pending.

valuable minutes, and in the aggregate *hours* of the employer's time. This notable abuse is obviated by the TIME REGISTER-ING CLOSET which completely and absolutely prevents an *enormous waste of valuable time with entire satisfaction* to both employer and employee.' It is all down to the 'G. W. Bowers Time Register'. In short, when someone goes to the loo, the clock starts ticking rather loudly, so that anyone can see how long the job takes, and wages can be deducted as appropriate. At the same time, for an extra $7.50, an extra device can be fitted to prevent two people going into the comfort station at the same time. And if the stay is for a period longer than five minutes, for a further $10.00, the employee can, by means of a compression system, be reduced to a small ball and flushed away.

Sewage No Value. The Sewage Difficulty Exploded
Edward Monson
n.p., 1874

The Kingdom of Dust
J. Gordon Ogden
Chicago, Ill.: Popular Mechanics, 1912

The Benefits of Farting Explain'd
Don Fart-inhando Puff-indorst (pseudonym – probably Jonathan Swift.)
13th edition, Printed for A. Moore, near St. Paul's, 1727
'With Additions revis'd by a College of Phyzz-icians, and approved by several Ladies of Quality.'

The Zen of Bowel Movements: A Spiritual Approach to Constipation
Kathy A. Price
Santa Barbara, Ca.: Rock House Pub., 1995

The B E N E F I T of

F A R T I N G

E X P L A I N ' D:

OR, THE

FUNDAMENT-all *C A U S E* of *the* *Diſtempers incident to the* Fair Sex.

Inquir'd into :

Proving *à Poſteriori* moſt of the *Diſordures* in·tail'd on, them are owing to *Flatulencies* not ſeaſonably vented.

Wrote in *Spaniſh*, by Don *Fart-in hand*o *Puff-in dorſt* Profeſſor of *Bumbaſt* in the Univerſity of *Craccow*.

A N D

Tranſlated into *Engliſh* at the Requeſt and for the Uſe of the Lady *Damp-Fart*, of *Her-fart-ſhire*.

A FART, tho' wholeſome does not fail,	*Thus Gun-powder confin'd, you know Sir,*
If barr'd of Paſſage by the Tail,	*Grows ſtronger, as 'tis ram'd the cloſer ;*
To fly back to the Head again,	*But, if in open Air it fires,*
And by its Fumes diſturb the Brain :	*In harmleſs Smoke its Force expires.*

The THIRTEENTH EDITION, *with Additions, revis'd by a College of* Phyzz-icians, *and approved by ſeveral Ladies of Quality.*

L O N D O N:

Printed for *A. Moore*, near St. *Paul's*, and Sold by the Bookſellers, 1727.

It's a Gas! A Study of Flatulence
Eric S. Rabkin and Eugene M. Silverman
Riverside, Ca.: Xenos Books, 1991

End Product
Daniel Sabbath and Mandel Hall
New York: Urizen Books, 1977

All About Mud
Oliver R. Selfridge
Reading, Mass.: Addison-Wesley, 1978

Dust and the Dustbin
Mrs Sheil
Home and Colonial School Society, n.d.
Mrs Sheil is described as 'Lecturer, for the Ladies' Sanitary Association and the National Health Society'.

Goodbye to the Flush Toilet: Water-Saving Alternatives to Cesspools, Septic Tanks and Sewers
Carol Hupping Stoner
Emmaus, Pa.: Rodale Press, 1984

Anaerobic Sludge Digestion
Task Force on Anaerobic Sludge Digestion
Alexandria, Va.: Water Pollution Control Federation, n.d.

Dangers to Health: A Pictorial Guide to Domestic Sanitary Defects
T. Pridgin Teale
J. and A. Churchill, 1878
In chapters with graphic titles such as 'How People Drink Sewage', Mr Teale describes in appalling detail the way in which undesirable ingredients are accidentally added to drinking water.

Constipation and Our Civilization
James Charles Thomson
Thorsons Publishers, 1943
'The connection between our Indigestion and our

Indecision; Our Food and our Behaviour. Advertising Specialists, Pain, Drugs and Enemas... I was discussing soured tissues with Henry Lynch, a Canadian engineer, at that time owner of the Marvel Cave in the Ozarks, Missouri, and also something of a biologist in his spare time...'

On the Composition of Farmyard Manure
Dr. Augustus Voelcker
Printed by W. Clowes and Sons, 1856
Voelcker took another dip into:
Liquid Manure
Printed by W. Clowes and Sons, 1859

Cleaning Up Coal
Gerhard Webber
New York: Harper and Row, 1982
If you think coal is nasty, dirty stuff, this is the book for you.

England's True Wealth
William White
Groombridge and Sons, 1849
The original binding is sumptuous green watered silk, lettered in gilt, *England's True Wealth*. It gives the clear impression of being a scarce pamphlet on banking or economics, probably by a wealthy politician rich enough to garb his random thoughts in an almost regal cloak. In fact, the full title on the title-page reads: *England's True Wealth; or Foecal Matters in Their Application to Agriculture by William White, Consulting Chemist to the City of London Portable Manure Company.*

8

THE WONDERFUL WORLD OF NATURE

Weird books on plants and animals

An Essay Towards the Character of the Late Chimpanzee, Who Died Feb. 23, 1738–9
Anon.
n.p., 1739

Performing Goats
Anon.
Pictures for Children, 1895

Sanitation and Anti-Fly Measures. The Life History of The Fly
Anon.
Issued by General Headquarters, 1917

Assessments and Decisions: A Study of Information Gathering by Hermit Crabs
Robert W. Elwood and S. J. Neil
Chapman and Hall, 1992

My Vagrant Vipers
Philip J. Baldensperger
Boy's Own Paper, 1912
Escaped snakes, and how Mr Baldensperger recaptured them.

Harnessing the Earthworm
Thomas J. Barrett
Faber and Faber, 1949

Blood Histamine Levels in Swine Following Total Body X-Radiation and a Flash Burn
Hamilton A. Baxter
Reprinted from Annals of Surgery, 1954

Development of the Female Genital Tract in the American Opossum
James S. Baxter
Washington, DC: Carnegie Institution of Washington, 1935

Fishes I Have Known
Arthur A. Henry Beavan
T. Fisher Unwin, 1905

Dung Fungi: an Illustrated Guide to Coprophilous Fungi in New Zealand
Ann Bell
Wellington: Victoria University Press, 1984

Bean Spasms
Ted Berrigan
New York: Kulchur Press, 1967

The Psychic Life of Micro-Organisms
Alfred Binet
Longmans and Co., 1889

Adventures with Small Animals
Owen Bishop
Murray, 1982

Black-Footed Ferret Recovery Plan
Black-Footed Ferret Recovery Team
Washington, DC: United States Fish and Wildlife Service, 1978

Animals as Criminals
J. Brand
Pearson's Magazine, 1896
'Murder is a common crime among parrots.'

The Story of a California Rabbit Drive
S. Ervin Chapman
New York: Fleming H. Revell, 1910
Comparison with a beetle drive would be erroneous: rabbits are herded into pens and then clubbed to death.

Frog Raising for Pleasure and Profit

Dr. Albert Broel

New Orleans, La.: Marlboro House, 1950

Broel, who is described as the 'Originator of Canned Frog Legs', provides the following extensive collection of recipes:

How do you want them?

Giant Frog Gumbo

Fried Frog Legs

Giant Frog Sandwich Spread

Fricassee [*sic*] of Giant Bullfrog

French Fried Giant Frog and Soup Colbert

Giant Bullfrog Cream Broth

Devilled Giant Bullfrog Meat

American Giant Bullfrog Cocktail

American Giant Bullfrog Pie, Country Style

Giant Bullfrog Mince Meat

Giant Bullfrogs Jellied

Giant Bullfrog Club House Sandwich

Giant Bullfrog Croquettes

Giant Bullfrog Meat with Dumplings

Grilled Giant Bullfrog Sandwich

Barbecued Giant Bullfrog Sandwiches

Giant Bullfrog Meat and Rice, Chinese Style

Giant Bullfrog Chop Suey

Jellied Giant Bullfrog Creamed Salad

Giant Bullfrog Salad
Dominant Mayonnaise
    Dressing for Giant Frogs
Giant Bullfrog Luncheon
    with Tomatoes
Giant Bullfrog Luncheon
    with Corn
Escalloped Giant Bullfrog
    with Celery and Potatoes
Giant Bullfrog à la King
Giant Bullfrog Pot Pie
Minced Giant Bullfrog
    Savory Sandwiches
Hot Giant Bullfrog
    Sandwiches with
    Newberg Sauce
Giant Bullfrog Meat
    Russian Sandwich
Giant Bullfrog Short Cakes
Giant Bullfrog Sandwich
    Loaf
Giant Bullfrog Pineapple
    Salad
Creamed Giant Bullfrog
    and Mushrooms
Giant Bullfrog Omelet
Stuffed Egg with Giant
    Bullfrog
Baked Apples stuffed with
    Giant Frog Meat
Stuffed Baked Tomatoes
    with Giant Bullfrogs

Hypnotising Animals
Hereward Carrington
New York: n.p., 1931

Psychology of Botany
'Charubel'
Tyldesley: R. Welch, 1906

The Common Teasel as a Carnivorous Plant
Miller Christy
Journal of Botany, 1922

Carnivorous Butterflies
Austin Hobart Clark
Washington, DC: United States Government Printing Office, 1926

Swine Judging for Beginners
Joel Simmonds Coffey
Columbus, Ohio: Ohio State University, 1915

Comprehensive Utilization of the Milk-thistle
The Editing Group of the 'Comprehensive Utilization of the Milk-thistle'
Beijing: Science Press, 1982

The Amateurs' Guide to the Study of the Genitalia of Lepidoptera
Peter W. Cribb
Orpington: Amateur Entomologist, 1973

Do Snakes Have Legs?
Bert Cunningham
New York: Reprinted from Scientific Monthly, 1934

Greek Insects
Malcolm Davies and Jeyaraney Kathirithamby
Oxford: Oxford University Press, 1986
'Written jointly by a classical scholar and an entomologist, this is an authoritative catalogue alphabetically arranged, of insect mentioned by ancient authors.'

New Guinea Tapeworms and Jewish Grandmothers
Robert S. Desowitz
New York: Norton, 1981

Ants and Some Other Insects: An Enquiry into the Psychic Powers of These Animals
Auguste Henri Forel
(translated by William Morton Wheeler)
Chicago, Ill.: The Open Court Publishing Co., 1904

The Supernatural History of Worms
Marion C. Fox
Friends' Book Centre, 2nd edition, 1931

Rats for Those Who Care
Susan Fox
Neptune City, NJ: TFH Publications, 1995

Show Biz Tricks for Cats: 30 Fun and Easy Tricks You Can Teach Your Cat
Anne Gordon and Steve Duno
Holbrook, Mass.: Adams Media, 1996

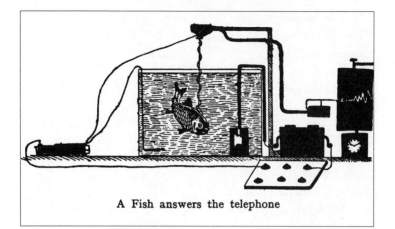

A Fish answers the telephone

Fish Who Answer the Telephone
Yury Petrovich Frolov
Kegan Paul, Trench, Trübner, 1937

The Ants of Colorado
Robert Edmond Gregg
Boulder, Colo.: University of Colorado Press, 1963

Ferret Facts and Fancies
A. R. Harding
Columbus, Ohio: The Author, 1915

Optical Chick Sexing
James E. Hartley and Ronald Hook
Nelson: Expert Chick Sexers, c.1954

Proceedings of the Second International Potato Modeling Conference
A. J. Haverkort and D. K. L. MacKerron (eds)
Dordrecht: Kluwer Academic Publishers, 1995

Fashion is Spinach
Elizabeth Hawes
New York: Random House, 1938

The Potatoes of Bolivia: Their Breeding Value and Evolutionary Relationships
J. G. Hawkes and J. P. Hjerting
Oxford: Clarendon Press, 1989

Male External Genitalia of Non-Prehensile Tailed South American Monkeys. Part I
Philip Hershkovitz
Chicago, Ill.: Field Museum of Natural History, 1993

The Goldfish of China in the 18th Century
George John Frangopulo Hervey
China Society, 1950

The Sleep of Plants
John Hill
Printed for R. Baldwin, 1757

Anaesthesia and Narcosis of Animals and Birds
Sir Frederick Thomas George Hobday
Baillière and Co., 1915

Hobday was also the author of:
Castration
Edinburgh: W. and A. K. Johnston, 2nd edition, 1914

Discovering the World of the Three-toed Sloth
John Hoke
Franklin Watts, 1976

Publicity is Broccoli
Constance Hope
Indianapolis, Ind.: Bobbs–Merrill, 1941

Did a Hen or an Egg Exist First? or, My Talks with a Sceptic
Jacob Horner
Religious Tract Society, c.1890

Predaceous Nematodes of Oregon
Harold James Jensen and Roland H. Mulvey
Corvallis, Oreg.: Oregon State University Press, 1968

Gigantic Cuttle-fish
William Saville Kent
Boston, Mass.: Estes and Lauriat, 1879

Digestion in the Pig
D. E. Kidder and M. J. Manners
Bath: John Wright, 1978

The Old Brown Dog: Women, Workers and Vivisection in Edwardian England
Coral Lansbury
Madison, Wis.: University of Wisconsin, 1985

Studies on Bunt or Stinking Smut
Robert Whilmer Leukel
Washington, DC: United States Department of Agriculture, 1937
A report on ways of reducing the incidence of these diseases of wheat crops.

Proceedings of the Fifteenth International Seaweed Symposium
Sandra C. Lindstrom and

David J. Chapman (eds)
Dordrecht: Kluwer Academic Publishers, 1996

Crab, Shrimp and Lobster Lore
William Barry Lord
George Routledge and Sons, 1867

Of the Irritability of Vegetables
Robert Lyall
Nicholson's Journal xxiv, 1809
There is nothing worse than a bad-tempered turnip.

A Veterinary Materia Medica and Clinical Repertory with a Materia Medica of the Nosodes
George Macleod
C. W. Daniel and Co., 1983

Favourite Flies and their Histories
Mary Orvis Marbury
Boston, Mass.: Charles T. Branford and Co., 1955

What Do Bunnies Do All Day?
Judy Mastrangelo
Nashville, Tenn.: Ideal Children's Books, 1988

The Home-Life and Economic Status of the Double-Crested Cormorant
Howard Lewis Mendall
Orono, Me.: University Press, 1936

A Short and Plain Explanation of Farmer Miles' Methods of Animal Castration and Spaying and After-treatment When Necessary
T. C. Miles
Charleston, Ill.: n.p., 1898

Swimming Sea Cucumbers… A Survey, with Analysis of Swimming Behavior
John E. Miller
Washington, DC: Smithsonian Institution Press, 1990

Memorandum on the Size, Sex and Condition of Lobsters
Ministry of Agriculture and Fisheries
HMSO, 1912
This report is described as being 'For Official Use' only. Full of interesting tables such as: 'Table (xii) – Number of Non-berried Lobsters Carrying Threads on Swimming Legs. Sussex, 1908-09.'

Pathobiology of the Ageing Rat
U. Mohr, D. L. Dungworth, and C. C. Capen (eds)
Washington, DC: International Life Sciences Institute, 1992

Characteristics of the Conditioned Response in Cretinous Rats
Garrett W. Morrison and Bert Cunningham
Baltimore, Md.: Reprinted from The Journal of Comparative Psychology, 1941

Gay Neck: The Story of a Pigeon
Dhan Gopal Mukerji
(Mukhopadhyaya Dhana-
Gopala)
Illustrated by Boris
Artzybasheff
J. M. Dent, 1928

The Joy of Chickens
Dennis Nolan
*Englewood Cliffs, NJ:
Prentice-Hall, 1981*
'A history and celebration
of the chicken, rare and
common.'
(Publisher's catalogue)

**Proceedings of the Second
International Workshop
on Nude Mice**
T. Nomura, N. Ohsawa, N.
Tamaoki and K. Fujiwara
(eds.)
*Tokyo: University of Tokyo
Press, 1978*

**Sexual Interactions in
Eukaryotic Microbes**
Danton H. O'Day and Paul
A. Horgen (eds.)
Academic Press, 1981

**The Giant Cabbage of the
Channel Islands**
Southcombe Parker and
G. Stevens Cox
*Guernsey Historical
Monograph No. 10, n.d.*

Dog Smugglers
Charles S. Pelham-Clinton
Strand Magazine, 1896
Showing how dogs are used
for smuggling tobacco from
Gibraltar to Spain.

**Life and Love in the
Aquarium**
C. H. Peters
*New York: Empire Tropical
Fish Import Co., 1934*

**International Symposium
on Developing the
Potentials of the Winged
Bean**
*Manila: Philippine Council
for Agriculture and Resources
Research, 1978*

Stress and Fish
A. D. Pickering (ed.)
Academic Press, 1981

The Genitalia of the British Pyrales with the Deltoids and Plumes: an account of the morphology of the male clasping organs of the female
F. N. Pierce and Frank Nelson
Farringdon: Classey, 1984

The Earthworms of Ontario
John W. Reynolds
Toronto: Royal Ontario Museum, 1977

Carrots Love Tomatoes
Louise Riotte
Charlotte, Vt.: Garden Way, 1981

Success with Small Fruits
Edward Payson Roe
New York, 1880

Bibliography of the Rhinoceros
L. C. Rookmaaker
Rotterdam: A. A. Balkema, 1983

Illustrated Catalogue of the Rothschild Collection of Fleas (Siphonaptera) in the British Museum (Natural History)
Miriam Rothschild, et al
Oxford University Press/British Museum (Natural History), 7 vols, 1953–

The History and Social Influence of the Potato
Redcliffe Nathan Salaman
Cambridge: Cambridge University Press, 1970

Fun with Land Hermit Crabs
Daniele Scermino
St Petersburg, Fla.: Palmetto Publishing Co., 1978

Enjoy Your Chameleon
Earl Schneider
New York: The Pet Library, n.d.

Thought Transference (or What?) in Birds
Edmund Selous
Constable, 1931; part 2, 1933

The Art of Faking Exhibition Poultry
George Ryley Scott
T. Werner Laurie, 1934
The author treads an indistinct line between condemning this widespread and despicable practice, and telling the reader exactly how to do it. It includes one crucial piece of advice: 'Always wear rubber gloves'.
Mr Scott also tells us:

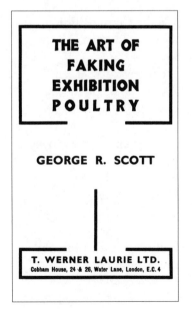

The Truth About Poultry
Poultry Press, 1927
With these two titles, Scott was taking a welcome break from his usual line of authorship: most of his published works are devoted to the subjects of nudism, birth control, flogging, capital punishment, torture, prostitution, obscene libel, sex guides and venereal disease.

Pigs on the Stage
Harold J. Shepstone
Royal Magazine, 1902
Including a carriage drawn by a pair of pigs and driven by a dog, a pig on a barrel, pigs on a seesaw, and a black hog 'enjoying a siesta in his rocking chair'.

Elements of the Organic Enamel of the Hedgehog
John Silness
Bergen: Universitetsforlaget, 1967

Birds Asleep
Alexander Frank Skutch
Austin: University of Texas Press, 1989

Birds Fighting
Stuart Smith and Eric Hosking
Faber and Faber, 1955
Photographs of birds attacking stuffed birds.

Marriage Rites of Orchids. Abstract of an Address to the Eleventh Anniversary Meeting of the Orchid Circle of Ceylon
Dr E. Soysa
Colombo: Printed at The Caxton Printing Works, c.1949
'Let us now witness the ceremonial of an ordinary Orchid wedding...'

The Genitalia of Bombyliidae
Oskar Theodor
Jerusalem: Israel Academy of Sciences and Humanities, 1983
'The genitalia were little noted by early authors... the female genitalia being completely disregarded...' (Publisher's catalogue).

Thirty Years of Bananas
Alex Makula
Nairobi: Oxford University Press, 1993

Mushrooms of Idaho
Edmund E. Tylutki
Moscow, Id.: University Press of Idaho, 1979

On the Composition of a Mangold-wurzel Kept for Two Years
Dr Augustus Voelcker
Printed by W. Clowes and Sons, 1859

Monograph of the Horny Sponges
R. Von Lendenfeld
Royal Society of London, 1889

Nutmeg Cultivation and the Sex-problem
H. Wageningen
Veenman and Zonen, 1966

Entomology in Sport
Hon. Mary Ward and Lady
Jane Mahon
Paul Jerrard and Son, 1859

**Comparative Studies of
the Psychology of Ants**
Eric Wasmann, SJ
St. Louis, Mo.: n.p., 1905

**The Cult of the
Budgerigar**
W. Watmough
Cage Birds, 1935

The Dog Orchestra
John West
n.p., 1897
'The property of Mr Louis
Lavater', featuring 'Jock the
trombone player, standing
on hind legs for half-an-
hour at a time', and Tim
the bass viol player who
'wears an almost painfully
sumptuous suit of bright
green satin'.

**The Longevity of Starved
Cockroaches**
Edwin R. Willis and
Norman Lewis

*Reprinted from The Journal of
Economic Entomology, 1957*

Spider Communication
Peter N. Witt and Jerome
S. Rovner (eds)
*Princeton, NJ: Princeton
University Press, 1982*

On Canine Madness
William Youatt
The Veterinarian, 1830

SPLAT!
Squashed creatures and
what to do with them.

**The Human Factor in
Game-Vehicle Accidents.
A Study of Drivers'
Information Acquisition**
Lars Aberg
*Stockholm: Almqvist and
Wiksell, 1981*
'The general purpose of the
present study is to study dif-
ferent aspects of human
behaviour in relation to
game-vehicle accidents in
general. The study has been

confined to accidents involving moose, mainly because the consequencies [*sic*] in general are more serious than those of other wildlife accidents.' (Publisher's catalogue)

Illinois Roadkill Cookbook
Bruce Carlson
Farmingdale, NY: Quixote Press Publications, 1990

What Bird Did That? A Driver's Guide to Some Common Birds of North America
Peter Hansard
Berkeley, Ca.: Ten Speed Press, 1991

That Gunk on Your Car
Mark E. Hostetler
Berkeley, Ca.: Ten Speed Press, 1997
A guide to the insects of North America and how to identify them from the patterns they make on your car windshield.

Flattened Fauna: A Field Guide to Common Animals of Roads, Streets, and Highways
Roger M. Knutson
Berkeley, Ca.: Ten Speed Press, 1987
'Why an animal is on the road and what it was doing there a few hours earlier are recorded in its flat remains as surely as the history of a tree is recorded in its annual rings.'

How to Cook Roadkill: Gourmet Cooking
Richard Marcou
Emeryville, Ca.: Publishers Group West, 1987

Feathers and Fur on the Turnpike
James Simmons
n.p., 1938

9

IN SICKNESS AND IN HEALTH

Medical oddities and sick titles

Exposure and Removal of the Brain
E. K. Adrian, Jr.
Health Series Consortium, 1984

Onania; or, The Heinous Sin of Self-Pollution, and all its Frightful Consequences, in Both Sexes, Considered
Anon.
The Author, 1725; 19th edition, 1759

A Pictorial Book of Tongue Coating
Anon.
Kyoto: Yukonsha Publishing Co., 1981
From the publishers of *A Complete Work of*

Acupuncture and Moxibustion (25 vols) comes a guide to the ancient Chinese method of diagnosis by examination of the tongue, which includes 257 coloured photographs of:

25: Whitish tongue with reddened tip and thick yellowish white greasy fur
63: Pink tongue with red spots, purple speckles and thin whitish greasy fur
139: Dull red furless tongue with scanty slobber
196: Deep red tongue with a slippery moist 'mouldy sauce paste' fur
217: Bluish purple lean small tongue with a white rotten fur

A Short Account of the Origin, Progress, and Present State of the New Rupture Society

Anon.
*Published by the Society,
Printed by S. Gosnell, 1816*

What to Do if it's Catching

Anon.
Sheffield: Newton, Chambers and Co., 1938

Old Age: Its Cause and Prevention

Sanford Bennett
New York: Physical Culture Publishing Co., 1912
The electric face mask recommended 'is wonderfully effective and it certainly does whiten the skin and generally improve the complexion. If accurately fitted it will last a life time'. Bennett is described as 'the man who grew young at 70'.

The woman in the iron mask demonstrates a ghastly alternative to growing old gracefully.

A Comparative View of the More Intimate Nature of Fever
James Black
Longman and Co., 1826

The Romance of Proctology
Charles Elton Blanchard
Youngstown, Ohio: Medical Success Press, 1938
'The story of the history and development of this much neglected branch of surgery from its earliest times to the present day, including brief biographic sketches of those who were its pioneers.'

Feeding Per Rectum: As Illustrated in the Case of the Late President Garfield and Others
D. W. Bliss, MD
Washington DC: The Author, 1882
Garfield survived for just over one month in 1881 by the use of nutritious enemata, mainly beef peptonoids.

Colon Cleanse the Easy Way!
Vena Burnett and Jennifer Weiss
New York: n.p., c.1979

Burr Identification System of Breast Analysis
Timothy Burr
Trenton, NJ: Hercules Publishing Co., 1965
This book is described as a scientific method of showing '...why and how women's breasts reveal their character', and includes '...a uniquely valuable dictionary-commentary on a thousand ways to describe women'.

On Cancer of the Scrotum in Chimney-sweeps and Others
Henry T. Butlin
British Medical Association, 1892

Memoranda on Noses
Frank Campbell
T. Richards, 1874

**Fresh Air and
How to Use It**
Thomas Spees Carrington
*New York: The National
Association for the Study and
Prevention of Tuberculosis,
1912*

**The Breath of Life; or,
Mal-respiration, and Its
Effects Upon the
Enjoyment and Life of
Man**
George Catlin
New York: John Wiley, 1861
The book was later reissued
as:
**Shut your Mouth and Save
your Life**
N. Trübner and Co., 1869

Surplus Fat
William Francis Christie
Heinemann, 1927

**Cluthe's Advice to the
Ruptured**
Charles Cluthe
*Bloomfield, NJ: Chas. Cluthe
and Sons (of the Cluthe
Rupture Institute), 71st edi-
tion, 1915*

'Quickly Cured, but Would
Feel Lost Without It…
Your truss cured me in
about six months but as I
feel lost without it, I am still
wearing it.'

The Glands of Destiny
Ivo Geikie Cobb
William Heinemann, 1927

**Skin Diseases for
Beginners**
Richard Bertram Coles and
Patrick David Clifford
Kinmont
H. K. Lewis and Co., 1957

**Cancer: Is the Dog the
Cause?**
Samuel Walter Cort
*John Bale, Sons and
Danielsson, 1933*
'He that keepeth a dog in
domestication breaketh a
fundamental law and shall
not know health… to keep
a dog, to cuddle, fondle,
stroke, kiss or be kissed by a
dog, is to invite disease and
death.' And it is not just
cancer: the dog is also the

prime cause of measles, new flu, tetanus, cerebrospinal meningitis, diphtheria and foot and mouth disease. Mr. Cort asks '…which shall survive, DOGANITY or HUMANITY?'

Notes Sur la Sodomie
Jean Paul Henry Coutagne
Lyons: H. Georg, 1880

The Solar Plexus or Abdominal Brain
Theron Q. Dumont
Chicago, Ill.: Advanced Thought Publishing Co., 1920

The Unfailing Efficacy of Medical Electricity in Imparting Health, Strength and Durable Vigour to Enfeebled Organs, Whether the Result of Natural Causes, Imprudences in Early Life or in Mature Age, by Means of the Electro-Galvanic Improved Patent Self-Adjusting Curative Appliance, or Ne Plus Ultra, &c.
Dr Lionel Elliott
The Author, 1868
'Author of the Popular Work on *The Complete and Permanent Cure of Spermatorrhoea, Syphilis, Gonorrhoea, Gleet, Stricture, &c, and the Granulation and Cicatrization of Ulcers and Deep Seated Wounds, &c, &c.*'

A Treatise on the Stomach and Its Trials
James Crossley Eno
Leeds, Newbery and Sons, 11th edition, 1881

'Yes; when I suffer from a
  brain overwrought –
Excited, feverish, worn,
  from laboured thought –
Harassed by anxious care,
  or sudden grief,
I run to Eno and obtain
  relief.'

Fatigue 96: Proceedings of the Sixth International Fatigue Congress
Oxford: Pergamon Press, 1996

The History of Cold Bathing
Sir John Floyer
S. Smith and B. Walford, 1706
Sir John was a great advocate of the cold dip and wrote several works on the subject. However, even he realises it is not always the right remedy:

"A Gentleman of the Temple, a hale man, of a strong athletick Habit... stayed in the cold bath of Mr Baynes at least 15 minutes... but it so chill'd him, that he had much ado to recover it, and was not well in some time...'

Secret of the Ring Muscles: Healing Yourself Through Sphincter Exercise
Paula Garbourg
Wayne, NJ: Avery Group, 1997

Sensors and Sensory Systems for an Electronic Nose
Julian W. Gardner and Philip N. Bartlett
Dordrecht: Kluwer Academic Publishers, 1992

How to Use the Veedee for Various Complaints
J. E. Garratt
The Author, c.1908
Garratt headed his personal notepaper 'The Veedee for Mechanical Massage', with his Cable Address 'Bronchial, London'. The book contains

a special chapter relating to uses of the Veedee in the toilet.

Spiritual Midwifery
Ina May Gaskin
Summertown, Tenn.: The Book Publishing Co., 1978

Therapy, Nudity and Joy: The Therapeutic Use of Nudity Through the Ages
Aileen Goodson
Los Angeles, Ca.: Elysium Books, 1990

Come Again, Nurse
Jane Grant
Robert Hale, 1960

Fingernail Biting: Theory, Research and Treatment
H. H. Hadley
Lancaster: MTP Press Ltd., 1983

The Handbook for Fitters of Camp Supports. With Anatomical Drawings by Tom Jones
Rhoda Grace Hendrick
Jackson, Mich.: S. H. Camp and Co., 1938

Scurvy: Past and Present
Alfred F. Hess
Academic Press, 1982

Sell Yourself to Science: The Complete Guide to Selling Your Organs, Body Fluids, Bodily Functions, and Being a Human Guinea Pig
Jim Hogshire
Port Townsend, Washington: Loompanics Unlimited, 1992

Imaging of the Scrotum: Textbook and Atlas
Hedvik Hricak, Bernd Hamm, and Bohyun Kim
New York: Raven Press, 1995

On Leprosy and Fish-eating: A Statement of Facts and Explanations
Sir Jonathan Hutchinson
Constable and Co., 1906

Inflammatory Bowel Diseases: A Personal View
H. D. Janowitz
Yearbook Medical Publishers, 1986

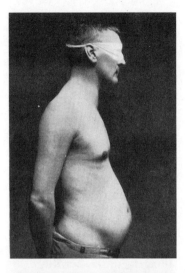

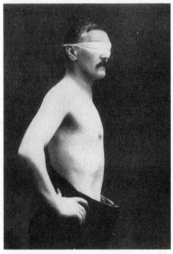

The cultured abdomen, before and after.

The Culture of the Abdomen, the Cure of Obesity and Constipation
F. A. Hornibrook
Heinemann, 1924
A classic that went to 11 editions between 1924 and 1937, cured Arnold Bennett of dyspepsia and gave H. G. Wells 'a new lease of life'.

The Sophisticated Shopper's Guide to Plastic Surgery
Richard Jobe
Rolling Hills Estates, Ca.: Robert Erdman Publishers, 1990

The Serious Lesson in Presidents Harding's Case of Gonorrhoea
E. Haldeman Julius
Girard, Ka.: Haldeman Julius, 'A Little Blue Book No.1580', 1931

De l'Amputation du Pénis
Louis Jullien
Paris: n.p., 1873

The Itinerary of a Breakfast
John Harvey Kellogg
New York: Funk and Wagnalls Co., 1926
'A popular account of the travels of a breakfast through the food tube and of the ten gates aad [*sic*] several stations through which it passes, also of the obstacles which it sometimes meets.'

You Can't Catch Diabetes from a Friend
Lynne Kipnis and Susan Adler
Gainsville, Fla.: Triad, 1979

The Art of Invigorating and Prolonging Life.... To which is Added The Pleasure of Making a Will
William Kitchiner
n.p., 1822
Dedicated to 'The Nervous and Bilious'.

Coma Arousal
Edward B. Le Winn
New York: Doubleday, 1985

The publishers advise that 'No special equipment or expertise is necessary'.

A Colour Atlas of Posterior Chamber Implants
Arthur S. M. Lim
Bristol: John Wright/P. G. Publishing, 1984
'A welcome and valuable new source of information.'
(Publisher's announcement)

The Romance of Leprosy
E. Mackerchar
The Mission to Lepers, 1949
'All down the ages the disease of leprosy has fascinated writer, artist, and poet, providing each in turn with themes upon which to exercise the loftiest imagination, and the highest artistic skill.'

The heights of romance are to be found in the brief biography of Mrs Gong, the Chinese bible-woman of Foochow:

'Without the least fear of the disease this intrepid

worker threw her whole soul and strength into the task allotted to her... the warning to avoid close contact with those to whom she ministered fell on deaf ears... Nine years passed and then the blow fell... "I never thought I would get it" was the pathetic remark of this brave sufferer.'

The Fountain of Youth; or, Curing by Water. How You May Quickly Overcome Acute and Chronic Illness by the Use of the Biological Blood-Washing Bath
Dr Benedict Lust
Introduction by Bernarr Macfadden
New York: Macfadden Publications, 1923
Bernarr Macfadden refers in his introduction to the unfortunately named Dr Lust's 'profound interest in Mr Christos Parasco's discovery' – a discovery which 'actually washes the poisons from the system'. The 'Technique of Rectal Irrigation' in 'The Knee-Chest Position' is apparently best, 'allowing from four to six pints of water to be injected safely and without inconvenience'. Macfadden, who was himself the author of *The Real Secret of Keeping Young* enjoyed a long life, celebrating his 83rd birthday by parachuting into the Hudson River. He died of jaundice at the age of 87.

Rectal irrigators Parasco and Lust mercifully use line-drawings to illustrate their techniques.

While this position can, in many cases, be held for a short time only, it shows a superior method for reaching the external pelvic organs, lower abdomen, inner surfaces of the thighs and the perineum—all closely associated with the sexual function and the health of the inner pelvic organs. After a few moments in this position the patient may assume the next position for a continuation to some extent of the same effect.

111

**Living Canvas:
A Romance of Aesthetic
Surgery**
Elisabeth Margetson
Methuen, 1936
Margetson was known
mainly for her Ward Lock
novels, including *Women are
Different* (1936), *A Kiss for a
Sailor* (1943), *Cancel All Our
Vows* (1944) and *Better to
Marry* (1946).

**From the Stump to the
Limb**
A. A. Marks
*New York: A. A. Marks and
Co., c.1890*
An illustrated history and
description of the artificial
limb company, with
testimonials: 'The hand
you made and sent me was
received in first class
condition...'

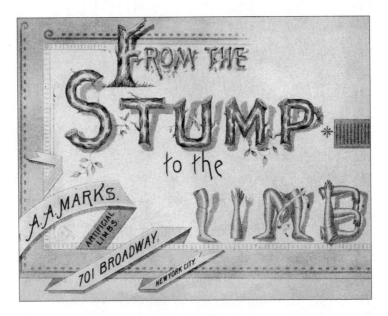

My Prostate and Me
William Curtis Martin
New York: Cadell and Davies, 1994

A Study of Masturbation and Its Reputed Sequelae
John Francis William Meagher
Baillière, Tindall and Cox, 1924
An enlightened approach – 'Any recommendation to marry in order to cure the habit is abominably bad and unfair'. The title of the second edition was altered to *A Study of Masturbation and the Psychosexual Life* (1929).

Practical Infectious Diseases
Richard D. Meyer
New York: John Wiley and Sons, 1983

Bournemouth in Lung Troubles
Vincent Milner
Baillière, Tindall and Cox, 1896

Three Weeks in Wet Sheets
'A Moist Visitor to Malvern'.
Hamilton, Adams, and Co., 1856

Troubles We Don't Talk About
Joseph Franklin Montague
Philadelphia, Pa.: J. B. Lippincott Co., 1927
The troubles Montague did not want to talk about were diseases of the rectum, but he was quite happy to discuss *mal de mer*, as in his:
Why Bring That Up? A Guide To and From Seasickness
New York: The Home Health Library, 1936

Guts
John Edward Morton
Baltimore, Md.: University Park Press, 1979

My Duodenal Ulcer and I
Dr Stuart Morton
(pseudonym of John Spence Meighan)
Christopher Johnson, 1955

**How to Conduct a
Magnetic Healing
Business**
A. C. Murphy
*Kansas City, Mo.: Hudson–
Kimberly, 1902*

**Electricity as a Cause of
Cholera, or Other
Epidemics, etc.**
Sir James Murray
Dublin: J. M'Glashan, 1849

**The Ethics of Medical
Homicide and Mutilation**
Austin O'Malley
*New York: The Devin–Adair
Co., 1922*

**The Abuse of Elderly
People: A Handbook for
Professionals**
Jacki Pritchard
J. Kingsley, 1992

A Paper on Yaws
J. Numa Rat
St Kitts: The Advertiser, 1902

**The Mesmeric Guide for
Family Use**
S. D. Saunders

H. Baillière, 1852
How to cure all known
diseases by hypnotizing
your spouse, children, etc.
Its fifty pages give concise
instructions on curing deaf-
ness, cancer, consumption
and the common cold.

**Backache, Birth and
Figure Relief by Self-
Revolving Hipbones**
William Schoenau
*Los Angeles, Ca.: The Author,
1951*
Printed on the title page is
the legend: 'The words
herein are all defined in
Webster's Dictionary'.

**Commentaries on the
Uses and Necessity of
Lavements in the
Correction of Habitual
Constipation, &c. through
the Sympathetic Relations
of the Lower Bowels**
James Scott
Churchill, 1830

A Study of Telegraphists' Cramp
May Smith, Millais Culpin, and Eric Farmer
Medical Research Council, Industrial Fatigue Research Board. HMSO, 1927

Injurious Effects of the Constant Use of Baby Carriages and Bicycles on the Physical Development of the Young
Henry Hollingsworth Smith
Philadelphia, Pa.: n.p., 1881

The Boy's Own Book of Health
William Gordon Stables
Jarrold and Sons, 1892
Contains a useful chapter on 'Pretty Men'.

Nasal Maintenance: Nursing your Nose through Troubled Times
William Alan Stuart
New York: McGraw-Hill, 1983

A Handbook of 'Chiropody' Giving the Causes and Treatment of Callosities, Bunions, Chilblains and the Diseases of the Toe-nails
Felix Wagner
Osborne, Garrett and Co., 1903
Extracted callosities and deformed big toes are to Mr. Wagner what stamps are to the philatelist, and the book is lavishly illustrated with mounted examples from his collection.

Syphilis: or, A Poetical History of the French Disease
N. Tate (translator)
For Jacob Tonson, 1686
The English translation of Girolamo Fracastoro's *Syphilis sive morbus Gallicus (Verona: n.p., 1530)* – the book that gave us the word 'syphilis'.

The Prostate: A Guide for Men and the Women Who Love Them
Patrick C. Walsh and Janet Farrar Worthington
Baltimore, Md.: Johns Hopkins University Press, 1995

Natural Bust Enlargement with Total Mind Power: How to Use the Other 90 Per Cent of Your Mind to Increase the Size of Your Breasts
Donald L. Wilson
Larkspur, Ca: Total Mind Power Institute, 1979

Put Hemorrhoids and Constipation Behind You
Kenneth B. Yasny
East Canaan, Conn.: Safe Goods, 1997

The Diagnosis of the Acute Abdomen in Rhyme
Zeta (pseudonym of Sir Vincent Zachary Cope)
H. K. Lewis, 1947

KEEP FIT

Mechanical Exercise A Means of Cure, Being a Description of the Zander Institute, London: Its History, Appliances, Scope and Object. Edited by the Medical Officer to the Institution
Anon.
J. and A. Churchill, 1883
An astonishing collection of machines designed to exercise one part of the body at a time, including 'Abduction' of the legs.

How to Pose as a Strong Man
W. Barton-Wright
Pearson's Magazine, 1899
'How, when lying at length on two chair backs placed at your extremities, to support a person standing on your chest.'

Text-book of Club Swinging
Tom Burrows
Health and Strength, 1908

Gus Hill's Champion Club-Swinging and Dumb-bell Manual: A complete guide by which any one can learn these healthy exercises, as it contains instructions in everything appertaining to these useful and beneficial accomplishments, together with the requirements and construction of the gymnasium
Gus Hill
New York: New York Popular Publishing Co., c.1880

Precursors of the home gym, two of the extraordinary devices from *Mechanical Exercise*, pioneered by the Zander Institute.

Fitness For All with the Wonder Ball
Edi Polz
Odhams, 1938
The author is described as 'The famous physical culture expert of international reputation'.

Exercise in the Bath
T. R. Togna
Putnam, 1938
Contains photographs of a bald man apparently going berserk in a bath.

A Sure Way to Lengthen Life with Vigor; Particularly in Old Age; the Result of Experience. Written by Dr Trusler at the Age of 84
John Trusler
Bath: T. Smith, 1819

JARM – How to Jog with your Arms to Live Longer
Joseph D. Wassersug
Port Washington, NY: Ashley Books, 1983
Within a year, the same publishers decided to present the opposing point of view with: *Jogging – The Dance of Death* by Robert Gene Fineberg. In the event of readers failing to achieve any discernible result from the aforementioned books, they are recommended to try the following:
How To Get Fat
Edward Smith
John Smith and Co., 1865
or
How To Be Plump
Thomas Cation Duncan
Chicago, Ill.: Duncan Bros., 1878

ON THE PSYCHIATRIST'S COUCH

**A Madman's Musings...
Written by A Patient
During his Detention in a
Private Madhouse**
Anon.
A. E. Harvey, n.d.

**On the Writing of the
Insane**
George Mackenzie Bacon
J. Churchill and Sons, 1870

**The Hive; or, Mental
Gatherings. For the
Benefit of the Idiot and
His Institution**
Eliza Grove
*Earlswood: The Asylum for
Idiots, 1857*

Fish's Schizophrenia
Max Hamilton
Bath: John Wright, 1984

**Wed To a Lunatic. A Wild,
Weird Yarn of Love and
Some Other Things
Delivered in the Form of**

**Hash for the Benefit of
Tired Readers**
Frank Warren Hastings
('Author of several widely
unknown works')
*St. Johnsbury, Vt.: L. W.
Rowell, 1896*
The second edition was
retitled:
Wed To a Lunatic. A Lie.
*St. Johnsbury, Vt.: The
Caledonian Press, 1901*
'Enlarged and revised to
meet the requirements of
modern science.'

**Let's Be Normal! The
Psychologist Comes to His
Senses**
Fritz Kuenkel
*New York: Ives Washburn,
1929*

**How to Become a
Schizophrenic**
John Modrow
*Everett, Wash.: Apollyon
Press, 1992*

I Knew 3,000 Lunatics
Victor Robert Small
*New York: Farrar and
Rinehart, 1935*

Synthetic Mania. By the author of 'Certified'. An Autobiographical Study
H. G. Woodley
Pen-In-Hand Publishing Co., 1948
'Madness is universal...'

The Maniac. A Realistic Study of Madness from the Maniac's Point of View
E. Thelmar
Watts and Co., 1909

Crook Frightfulness
'A Victim'
Birmingham: Cornish, 1932; Birmingham: Moody Bros., revised edition, 1935
The author of this book, identified only as 'A Victim', recounts the story of his life as a rent collector in the East End of London, in New Zealand and the West Indies. *Crook Frightfulness* is the autobiography of a hunted man who believes himself to be continually hounded and molested by evil men, or 'crooks'.

'How was I to know that I had of my own volition opened the doors of Hell – to turn me from a cheery, care-free youth of 18 to a prematurely aged man, terrified by horrible men, threatening my sanity and life?'

'I have had experiences which suggest crooks sometimes use a stethoscope apparatus which enables them to hear your thoughts.' He also provides

Crook Frightfulness
(REVISED)

By a Victim

They are the most powerful, terrible and pitiless killers, cunning, amazingly and enormously treacherous.

The serpent . . . more subtle than any.
Genesis iii. 1.

MOODY BROTHERS, LTD.
34, LIVERY STREET,
BIRMINGHAM, ENGLAND.

'I had just bidden adieu to a friend on the Aberystwyth Marine Parade and had just turned away from him when I heard the words – "The old sod" – said in my voice tones too!'

IN THE DENTIST'S CHAIR

History of Dentistry in Oregon
W. Claude Adams
Portland, Oreg.: Binfords and Mort, 1956

Why Replace a Missing Back Tooth?
Joel M. Berns
Kingston on Thames: Quintessence Publishing, 1987

Dentologia: A Poem on the Diseases of the Teeth and Their Proper Remedies
Solyman Brown (pseudonym of Eleazar Parmly)
New York: American Library of Dental Science, 1840

a detailed account of what he describes as 'ventriloquial terrorism', whereby '…a molestor using ventriloquism may be in a house or building or walking along in a tram or bus or in a car, yet he can throw his voice anywhere undetected by those who are near them.' This technique gives rise to various embarrassing experiences, including one where

'On a subject so unpromising,
I think all would agree with
me in saying that the author
has succeeded beyond all
reasonable expectations.
Derangement, pain and
    swift decay,
Obtain in man their
    desolating sway,
Corrupt his blood, infect his
    vital breath,
And urge him headlong to
    the shades of death.'

Psychiatric Disorders in Dental Practice
Morgan David Enoch and
Robert G. Jagger
Oxford: John Wright, 1994

Tooth Mutilations and Dentistry in Pre-Columbian Mexico
S. Fastlicht
*Kingston on Thames:
Quintessence Publishing, 1986*

New National Strength Through the Beauty of the Teeth
Henry C. Ferris
New York: The Author, 1919

The Dynamics of Psychosomatic Dentistry
Joseph S. Landa
*Brooklyn, NY: Dental Interest
Publishing Co., 1953*

The Dentist in Art
Jens Jorgen Pindborg and
L. Marvitz
George Proffer, 1961

Book-Keeping for Dentists
Frank 'Chalky' White
*Baillière, Tindall and Cox,
1910*
Credit for advice is also
extended to Eustace B. L.
White, and whiter-than-
white accounts and teeth are
guaranteed to all readers.

The Strange Story of False Teeth
John Woodforde
*Routledge and Kegan Paul,
1968*

10

LOVE, MARRIAGE AND...

Encounters, exotic and erotic

SEVEN WIVES

AND

SEVEN PRISONS:

OR

EXPERIENCES IN THE LIFE

OF A

MATRIMONIAL MONOMANIAC.

A TRUE STORY,

WRITTEN BY HIMSELF.

(A. 1880-?)

NEW YORK:
PUBLISHED FOR THE AUTHOR.
1870.

MY FIRST AND WORST WIFE

Seven Wives and Seven Prisons; or, Experiences in the Life of a Matrimonial Monomaniac. A True Story Written by Himself

L. A. Abbott
New York: The Author,
1870
The frontispiece portrait is of 'My first and worst wife'.

Love, Woman, Marriage: The Grand Secret

Anon.

Boston, Mass.: Randolph Publishing Co., 1871

'No description, critique, or synopsis can do justice to this mighty work, which ought to be bound in gold and be on the table of every man, woman and youth in the land and in the world. It is an exhaustive and large work.' (Publisher's description)

Literature of Kissing

Charles C. Bombaugh

Philadelphia, Pa.: J. B. Lippincott, 1876

Sex + Sex = Gruppensex

Ruediger Bosschmann

Flensburg: Stephenson Verlag, 1970

Bosschmann was also the author of:

Orgasmus und Super-Orgasmus

Flensburg: Stephenson Verlag, 1972

Brodie's Medical Work on Virility

The Authors

R. J. Brodie and Co., c.1844

Required reading before progressing to:

The Secret Companion, a Medical Work on Onanism

The Authors,

R. J. Brodie and Co., 1845

Sexual Analysis of Dickens' Props

Arthur Washburn Brown

New York: Emerson Books, 1971

Dickens reduced to a Freudian nightmare of sexual fantasy in 'a work inspired by Susanna Nobbe':

Why cribbage represents sexual intercourse

The erotic meaning of wooden legs

Erotic umbrellas and sexually suggestive food

Beanstalk Country: On top of the tallest erection

Is the Pleasure Worth the Penalty? A Common-sense View of the Leading Vice of the Age
Henry Butter
Job Caudwell, 1866

How to Speak and Write to Girls for Friendship
B. A. Chinaka
Onitsha: Njoku and Sons Bookshop, c.1963

Traps for the Young
Anthony Comstock
New York: Funk and Wagnalls, 1883
A spotter's guide to enable the confiscation of 'immoral literature' before it gets into the wrong hands.

Trial By Impotence: Virility or Marriage in Pre-Revolutionary France
P. Darmon
Chatto and Windus, n.d.

Women Around Hitler
Randolph S. Davies
E. Newman, Know Thine Enemy series, c.1943

'One of his women, when asked why her friendship with Hitler came to an end, said that she had a disappointment with him which did not redound to his advantage.'

The Girdle of Chastity
Eric John Dingwall
George Routledge and Sons, 1931
The definitive book on chastity belts.

Sexual Behaviour of the American Women
Govind Sadasiva Ghuyre
Bombay: Thacker, 1975

Wife Battering: A Systems Theory Approach
Jean Giles-Sims
Guilford Press, 1983

Office Gynecology
Jacob Pearl Greenhill
Chicago: Year Book Medical Publishers, 9th edition, 1971
There is another book with same title by Morton A. Stenchever (St Louis, Mo.: Mosby, 2nd edition, 1996).

Penis Enlargement Facts and Fallacies
Gary M. Griffin and Gary Rheinschild
Aptos, Ca.: Hourglass Book Publishers, 1995

Straight Talk About Surgical Penis Enlargement
Gary M. Griffin
Los Angeles, Ca.: Added Dimensions, 1993

Encyclopaedia of Sexual Knowledge
Doctors Haire, Costler, and Willy
Encyclopaedic Press, 1934

How To Be Happy Though Married
Rev. Edward J. Hardy
T. Fisher Unwin, 1885
'To those brave men and women who have ventured, or intend to venture, into that state which is "a blessing to a few, a curse to many, and a great uncertainty to all", this book is dedicated in admiration of their courage.'

How to Pick Up More Girls
Rory Harrity
Modern Age, 1972
If this doesn't work, try:
How to Pick Up Girls on Public Beaches
Raleigh Leo Stanley
Great Neck, NY: Todd and Honeywell, 1982
...or failing that:

How to Pick Up Women in Discos
Don Diebel
Houston, Tx.: Gemini Publishing Co., 1981

How to Love Every Minute of Your Life
Gay Hendricks and Carol Leavenworth
Englewood Cliffs, NJ: Prentice-Hall, 1978

How to Forgive Your Ex-husband
Marcia Hootman and Patt Perkins
New York: Doubleday, 1983

The White Women's Protective Ordinance: Sexual Anxiety and Politics in Papua
Amirah Inglis
Sussex University and Chatto and Windus, 1975

Male Sexuality: The Atlantis Position
Jenny James
Caliban Books, 1982

Training of the Young in Laws of Sex
Hon. Edward Lyttelton
Longman, 1900
'Strength of appetite' in a child of ten or eleven suggests, according to the author, that 'physical temptation later will be very strong'. This is the only sure symptom that a boy is 'contracting the habit' of 'this particular foe'. Lyttelton was also the author of:
The Causes and Prevention of Immorality in Schools
The Social Purity Alliance, 1887

Be Married and Like It
Bernarr Macfadden
New York: Macfadden Book Co., 1937
Macfadden was also the author of:
How Can I Get Married?
New York: Macfadden Publications, 1927
Subtitled 'A Woman Bares Her Soul: Vividly and Dramatically she tells the

Story of her Heart-Stirring Experience in her Search for a Husband'.
as well as
A Strenuous Lover: A Romance of a Natural Love's Vast Power
New York: Physical Culture Publishing Co., 1904
and
The Power and Beauty of Superb Womanhood. How they are Lost and How they May be Regained
New York: Physical Culture Publishing Co., 1901

The Breathless Orgasm: A Lovemap Biography of Asphyxiophilia
John Money, Gordon Wainwright, and David Hinsburger
Buffalo, NY: Prometheus Books, 1991

Brass Checks and Red Lights: Being a Pictorial Potpourri of Prostitutes, Parlor Houses, Professors, Procuresses, and Pimps
Fred and Jo Mazzulla

Denver, Co.: The Authors, 1966
An illustrated 'Who Was Who in Whoredom', based on the authors' collection, which includes pictures of the brass tokens used by prostitutes, such as that issued by Rith Jacobs, proprietor of the Silver Dollar Hotel, Denver, with the subtle inscription 'Good for One Screw'. Some bear the nicknames of the young ladies: 'Velvety Ass Rose', 'Few Clothes Molly', and 'Three-Tit Tillie' (who may or may not be the same Tillie as 'Two Ton Tillie', a token for 'Two Ton Three-Tit Tillie' having not yet been located). The Mazzulla Collection is now in the Amon Carter Museum, Fort Worth, Texas.

Scenes of Seduction: Prostitution, Hysteria and Reading Difference in Nineteenth Century France
Jann Matlock
New York: Columbia University Press, 1994

Homosexuality and Male Bonding in Pre-Nazi Germany: The Gay Movement, and Male Bonding Before Hitler's Rise
Harry Oosterhuis
New York: Harrington Park Press, 1991

The Sex Practitioner: A Step by Step Guide to the Pleasures of Sex
Harry Prick
New York: I. M. Horny, 1945
According to the National Union Catalog, there is only one recorded copy of this title (in the library of the University of Oregon, Eugene), catalogued, we assume, when the librarian's wife had been away on an extended vacation.

Stop in the Name of Love: Ejaculation Control for Life
Michael Riskin
Encino, Ca.: Choice Publishers, 1994

Erectile Disorders: Assessment and Treatment
Raymond C. Rosen and Sandra R. Leiblum
New York: Guildford Press, 1992
Described by a reviewer as 'filling a sizeable gap'.

Sex Life of the Foot and Shoe
William A. Rossi
New York: Saturday Review Press, 1976

Teach Yourself Sex
William Ewart Sargent
English Universities Press, 1951

The Causes of Infidelity Removed
Rev. Stephen Smith
Utica, NY: Grosh and Hutchinson, 1839

The Story of a Terrible Life: The Amazing Career of a Notorious Procuress
Basil Tozer
T. Werner Laurie, 1924
Tozer is described as

'Author of *Recollections of a Rolling Stone, Around the World with a Millionaire, The Irony of Marriage*, etc'.

Vital Force; or, Evils and Remedies of Perverted Sexuality. Shewing how the health, strength, energy, and beauty of human beings are wasted and how preserved
R. B. D. Wells ('Practical Phrenologist of Observatory Villa, West Bank, Scarborough')
Oldham: 16th Edition, thoroughly revised and enlarged, H. Vickers, &c., 1878
Classic 'should bad thoughts occur, take to some hard physical exercise' approach, with illustrations of a 'masturbator, smoker, and drinker' and a 'dull and obtuse condition of body and brain, produced by masturbation and smoking'. The link with smoking is straightforward: 'Nicotine powerfully affects the brain,

VITAL FORCE;

OR,

EVILS AND REMEDIES

OF

PERVERTED SEXUALITY.

SHEWING

HOW THE HEALTH, STRENGTH, ENERGY, AND
BEAUTY OF HUMAN BEINGS ARE WASTED,
AND HOW PRESERVED.

BY

R. B. D. WELLS, PRACTICAL PHRENOLOGIST,
AND HYGIENIC PRACTITIONER.

The "Hydro" West Bank, Scarborough.

SEVENTEENTH EDITION.
THOROUGHLY REVISED AND ENLARGED.

LONDON:
H. VICKERS, 317, STRAND.
MANCHESTER: JOHN HEYWOOD, DEANSGATE.
GLASGOW: JAMES COATES, PHRENOLOGIST.
NEWCASTLE-ON-TYNE, W. H. ROBINSON, BOOK MARKET.
LIVERPOOL: H. PROCTOR, 65, MOUNT PLEASANT.
SCARBOROUGH: R. B. D. WELLS, WEST BANK.

and the cerebellum which is the seat of the affections, becomes congested or inflamed; this in turn irritates the genital parts, produces sexual excitability, and conduces to masturbation. This latter in turn draws the blood and electricity from the brain and other parts of the body to the genital organs, and creates an abnormal craving for something which neither food nor natural drink can appease.'

DEVIANT DIVERSIONS

Peculiar pastimes

There is no end to the number of ways people choose to spend their spare time, and no end to the number of books published to help them. In this chapter, we have focused on Leisure Activities (including crafts, hobbies, and conjuring), Sport, Cookery and Travel.

LEISURE ACTIVITIES

Collect Fungi on Stamps
D. J. Aggersberg
Gibbons, 1997

Pole Stars. Some Extraordinary Performances on a Pole
H. L. Adam
n.p., 1902
Featuring De Witt and Burns, 'Perch Equilibrists', performing on a mast 100 feet high.

Fun with a Newspaper
Morley Adams
London Magazine, 1910
'All you need is three newspapers and a table.'

How to Eat a Peanut
Anon.
New York: n.p., c.1900

How to Vamp Without Music
Anon.
J. F. Dallas, 1943

Magic in India
Anon.
Edinburgh: n.p., 1852
With an illustration of a
snake-charmer whistling
Auld Lang Syne.

**Ten Good Tricks With
Empty Bass Bottles**
Anon.
*Burton-on-Trent: Bass,
Ratcliff and Gretton, 1929*
Includes 'The Hypnotised
Bottle'.

**The Great Pantyhose
Crafts Book**
Ed and Stevie Baldwin
*New York: Western
Publishing Co., Inc., 1982*
This book gives patterns for
forty different articles that
can be made from old
tights, starting with 'gifts
and bazaar [*sic*] items for
everyone'.

'Little Black Evening
Bag – If you've always
admired the evening purses
in the stores but hated to
spend the money, then this
project is for you!'

'The perfect touch… for
your home decor' can be created in the shape of a life-size
stuffed 'granny', and 'shady
lady', while the pantyhose
cactus 'is sure to be a conversation piece' and 'requires
even less care than a real one'.
And for that 'sparkling addition to a special occasion' the
Thanksgiving Turkey will be
'a decorative addition to your
Thanksgiving table – or tuck
a brick inside and use him as
a unique door stop'.

**Master Pieces: Making
Furniture from Paintings**
Richard Ball and Peter
Campbell
Poole: Blandford 1983

**Practical Taxidermy and
Home Decoration**
Joseph H. Batty
New York: Orange Judd, 1880

**Picture Your Dog in
Needlework**
B. Borssuck and Ann Jackson
*New York: Arco Publishers,
1980*

Dinkum Magic
J. Albert Briggs
Alexandria, New South Wales: The Austral Magic Co., 1928

Artists in Rags
Horace F. Burton
Royal Magazine, 1901
'Showing how, in default of paint, pictures may be made out of rags.'

Pranks with the Mouth
'W. C.'
Chamber's Journal, 1879
More serious than your average pranksters, the individuals featured here swallow knives, bayonets and swords.

The Man with the Iron Eyebrows
Edouard Charles
Royal Magazine, 1902
Mr. Gregor Olivos
'… screws his eyebrows between the two horizontal steel bars of the apparatus, enabling him to lift 244 lbs'.

The Art of Making Faces
J. R. Creed
Pearson's Magazine, 1897
Featuring 'Mr Walter Churcher, facial contortionist'.

How to Make Your Own Woodcarving Tools from Nails, Hacksaw Blades and Umbrella Ribs
Jack Van Deckter
New York: Venturecraft Kits Co., 1984

Foolhardy Feats
George Dollar
Strand, 1897
Featuring 'Kilpatrick, the one-legged cyclist'.

In Love and Unity. A Book About Brushmaking
Thomas Girtin
Hutchinson, 1961

Teach Yourself Alcoholism
Meier Glatt
EUP, 1975

Let's Make Some Undies
Marion Hall
W. Foulsham and Co., 1954
In the *Let's Make It* series.

The Art of Chapeaugraphy
John G. Hamley
C. Routledge, 1923
The long-awaited sequel to:
**Chapeaugraphy; or,
Twenty-Five Heads Under
One Hat**
W. and F. Hamley, c.1885

**The Champion Orange
Peeler**
A. B. Henn

Strand, 1899
The author, a ship's cook,
demonstrates how to make
extraordinary patterns, faces,
crowns, animals, and
pyramids out of orange peel.

**How to Pick Pockets.
A Treatise on the
Fundamental Principle,
Theory and Practice of
Picking Pockets**
Eddie Joseph
The Vampire Press, 1946
Joseph was also the
author of:
**How To Do Cups and
Balls**
The Vampire Press, 1946

Learn to Croon
Brand Larkin
W. Foulsham and Co., 1936

Macramé Gnomes
Dona Z. Meilach
*New York: Crown Publishers,
1980*

Levitation for Terrestrials
Robert Kingley Morison (ed.)
Ascent, 1977

The Projection of the Astral Body
Sylvan Joseph Muldoon and Hereward Carrington
Rider and Co., 1929

Suggestive Handwork for Lower Classes
Arthur B. Neal
Sir Isaac Pitman and Sons, 1905

Searching for Railway Telegraph Insulators
W. Keith Neal
St Saviours, Guernsey: The Signal Box Press, 1982
and its sequel:
Railway and Other Rare Insulators
St Saviours, Guernsey: The Signal Box Press, 1987

Frolic and Fun with Egg-Shells
Meredith Nugent
Girl's Realm, 1903
'After trying some of the schemes here suggested, you will find the fun is not only rolicking, but well nigh inexhaustible.' Fun-loving

Mr Nugent went on to tell his readers:
How to Have Fun with Old Newspapers
Girl's Realm, 1903

A Boiling Kettle and a Working Steamboat Made of Paper
Louis Nikola
Strand, 1905

Rope Spinning
D. W. Pinkney
Herbert Jenkins, 1930

Mr Pinkney prepares to become a Scout in Bondage.

You Can Make a Stradivarius Violin
Joseph V. Reid
Chicago, Ill.: Popular Mechanics Press, 1950 and 1955
Mr Reid is not a professional violin-maker; he is an engineer employed by the American Can Company of Canada. 'With experience anyone can make two violins a year and still play golf and fish.' He threatens that he '…may next take up Duncan Phyfe

furniture'. Copies are incomplete unless they contain the working drawings, and the loosely inserted errata slip noting errors in the location dimensions for the bass bar.

Build Your Own Hindenburg
Alan Rose
New York: Putnam, 1983

Hypnotism As It Is
Lamot Sage
Rochester, NY: New York Institute of Science, 6th edition, 1900
Among the examples illustrated are a '…subject in complete state of anaesthesia having ordinary steel hat pins pushed through his arm and face', and '…hypnotised young men [who] believe themselves to be darkies participating in a great cake walk'.

**The Passionate Game:
Lessons in Chess
and Love**
Gustav Schenk
G. Routledge and Son, 1937
The first principles of chess
as explained in a series of
love-letters – or is it the
other way round?

Spirit Rapping Made Easy
Dion Sweird
Felix McGlennan, 1926
This textbook is designed to
ensure a medium level of
success.

**Explosive Spiders and
How to Make Them**
John Scoffern
Boy's Own Paper, 1881
Pyrotechnicist Scoffern
shows how to manufacture
an '…artificial spider that,
when touched, should go off
with a bang'. A deluge of
complaints from parents
followed, but undaunted he
went on to write:
**Firework Pie
for a Picnic**
Boy's Own Paper, 1882

Folding Table Napkins
Mariane Van Borstedt and
Ulla Prytz
*Stockholm: ICA Forlaget,
1968*

**Original Tricks with
Cigars**
James Wakefield
Derby: The Author, 1927

Fun with Knotting String
Heidy Willsmore
Kaye and Ward, 1977

SPORTING LIFE

How to Twirl a Baton
Anon.
Chicago, Ill.: Ludwig and Ludwig, c.1930

How to Walk
Anon.
Evening News, 1903

Wrestling for Gay Guys
Donald Black
Power Books, 1994
'For those thinking about taking up wresting – whether for fun, fitness, self-defence, safe expression of anger or erotic stimulation... (see inside back cover).'

Tricks of Self-Defence. A Useful Book for Everybody
W. H. Collingridge
Health and Strength Ltd., 1914
The 10th edition, revised by Percy Longhurst, was issued in 1949.

Catching a Cannon Ball
Walter Brown Gibson
St Louis, Mo.: n.p., 1923

The Mystery of Golf
Theodore Arnold Haultain
New York: Macmillan, 1910

How You Can Bowl Better Using Self-hypnosis
Jack Heise
Wilshire, n.d.

Ball-Hopping Extraordinary
Frank Holmfield
Windsor Magazine, 1902
How to create sound-effects – marching soldiers, distant guns, and a train – and complex patterns of juggling by bouncing balls off floors and walls.

The New 'Soccer' Football Game
Ho-Mo
n.p., 1932

Side and Screw, Being Notes on the Theory and Practise of the Game of Billiards
Charles Dealtry Locock
Longmans, 1901

Knight Life: Jousting in the United States
Robert L. Loeffelbein
Lexington Park, Md.: Golden Owl, 1978

Knife Throwing: A Practical Guide
Harry K. McEvoy
Rutland, Vt.: Charles E. Tuttle Co., 1973

The Unwritten Laws of Fox-Hunting. Notes on the Use of the Horn and the Whistle, and List of 5,000 Names of Hounds
C. F. P. McNeill
Vinton and Co., 1911

Hand Grenade Throwing as a College Sport
Lewis Omer
New York: A. G. Spalding and Bros., 1918

The British Library's copy has unfortunately been 'Destroyed by bombing'.

Jerks In From Short Leg
'Quid' (pseudonym of Robert Allan Fitzgerald)
Harrison, 1866

Play With Your Own Marbles
J. J. Wright
S. W. Partridge, c.1865

'While Dick knelt down, ready to fire, Syl could not help but clutch his wonderfully-got bag of marbles all the tighter.'

Fun on the Billiard Table
'Stancliffe'
C. Arthur Pearson, 1899
From the author who
brought us:
**The Autobiography of a
Caddy-Bag**
Methuen, 1924

**The Secret Arts of Chinese
Leg Manoeuvres in
Pictures**
Lee Ying-Arng
n.p., n.d.

COOKING THE BOOKS

**The Sexual Politics of
Meat. A Feminist-
Vegetarian Critical Theory**
Carol J. Adams
*New York: Continuum
Publishing Co., 1990*

**The Life and Cuisine of
Elvis Presley**
David Adler
New York: Crown, 1993

Eatable Ghosts
Anon.
n.p., 1863

**The History of a Cup of
Tea in Rhymes and
Pictures**
Anon.
n.p., 1860

Les Gourmets au Congo
Anon.
*Antwerp: J. F. Buschmann,
n.d.*

Radiation Cookery Book
Anon.
*Birmingham: Radiation,
1927*

**Report of the Temperature
Reached in Army Biscuits
During Baking, Especially
with Reference to the
Destruction of the
Imported Flour-Moth
Ephestia Kuhnelia Zeller**
Anon.
*Journal of the Royal Army
Medical Corps, 1913*

Some Interesting Facts about Margarine
Anon.
n.p., n.d.
Does the title suggest that certain facts about margarine are *not* interesting?

Be Bold with Bananas
Australian Banana Growers Council
New York: Crescent Books, c.1970

Handlining and Squid Jigging
Bjorn A. Bjarnason
Rome: FAO, 1992

Cameos of Vegetarian Literature
Charles W. Forward (ed.)
The Ideal Publishing Union, 1898
Vegetarian Jubilee Library Vol. VIII. Includes 'The Slaughter of Animals for Food' by Henry S. Salt, and 'The Turnip in Sickness and Health' by Doris Y. Pepper.

How I Lived on 4¾ d. a Day. By a Woman Who Now Realizes that She Has Hitherto Eaten too Much
Janetta Griffiths Foulkes
Truslove and Bray, c.1912

Pernicious Pork; or, Astounding Revelations of the Evil Effects of Eating Swine Flesh
William T. Hallett
New York: Broadway Publishing Co., 1903

Ice Cream for Small Plants
Etta H. Handy
Chicago, Ill.: Hotel Monthly Press, 1937

Eat Your House: Art Eco Guide to Self-sufficiency
Frederic Hobbs
Carmel, Ca.: Virginia City Restoration Corporation, 1980

Everybody's Favorite Orthomolecular Muffin Book
Rose Hoffer
New Canaan, Conn.: Keats Publishing, 1980

The Complete Book of Bacon
William J. Hogan
Northwood Books, 1978

Bake a Snake: How to Survive Your Own Cooking in the Wilderness, in Camp, or at Home
Gerald Hunter
Wake Forest, NC: Meridional Publishing, 1981

Food for Survival After a Disaster. With Plates
Raymond Charles Hutchinson
Carlton: Melbourne University Press, 1959

Dainty Dishes for Slender Incomes
'Isobel' of Home Notes
C. Arthur Pearson, 1895
The 'dainty dishes' deemed suitable for those with 'slender incomes' include such modest fare as 'Turbot in Lobster Sauce', 'Duck and Salad', 'Soles à la Normande', and 'Grouse and Chips'.

The Anthropologists' Cookbook
Jessica Kuper (ed.)
New York: Universe Books, 1977
Includes a tasty roast-dog recipe from Ponape.

The Thermodynamics of Pizza
Harold J. Morowitz
New Brunswick, NJ: Rutgers University Press, 1991

About Yogurt
P. E. Norris
Thorsons Publishers, 1954; 10th impression, 1971
'Zaro Agha, a Turk, lived to be 162. He ate enormous quantities of yogurt all his life.'

Dangerous Cocoa; or, The Perils of Kola
'Quaestor'
James Hutcheson Hogg, c.1898

Cold Meat and How to Disguise It
Mrs M. E. Rattray
C. Arthur Pearson, 1904

What To Do with Cold Mutton: a Book of Réchauffés
Mary Renny
Richard Bentley and Son, 1887
First published in 1863 under the pseudonym 'A Gentleman of Moderate Means'.

Unmentionable Cuisine
Calvin W. Schwabe
Charlottesville, Va.: University Press of Virginia, 1979
Containing recipes for stewed cat, silk-worm omelette and red-ant chutney.

Miss Smallwood's Goodies. Easy Sweetmeat Making at Home
M. Smallwood
Manchester: The Author, 2nd edition, c.1890
'If food is the way to a man's heart, there is no doubt that any man would want to get his hands on Miss Smallwood's Goodies.'

Soyer's Paper Bag Cookery
Nicolas Soyer
Andrew Melrose, 1911

Entertaining with Insects; or, The Original Guide to Insect Cookery
Ronald L. Taylor and Barbara J. Carter (illustrated by John Gregory Tweed)
Santa Barbara, Ca.: Woodbridge Press Publishing Co., 1976

Miss Smallwood's

GOODIES

EASY SWEETMEAT MAKING
——AT HOME.——

[2nd Edition.   *Revised and Enlarged*].

By the Author of
" TABLE DELICACIES."

First-class Diplomée.

Lecturer Cape Town International and Industrial
Exhibition, 1904-5, and other Exhibitions.

[COPYRIGHT].

Living Without Eating
Herbert Thurston
Reprinted from The Month,
1931
Among the feats of 'famous
fasting girls' described by
Mr Newman are the '...five
years' unbroken fast by
Therese Neumann of
Konnersreuth, Bavaria'.

**The 120-Year Diet:
How to Double Your Vital
Years**
Roy L. Walford
*New York: Simon and
Schuster, 1986*

Appealing Potatoes
Princess Weikersheim
Hutchinson, 1981

**The Book of Marmalade:
Its Antecedents, Its
History and Its Role in the
World Today**
C. Anne Wilson
Constable, 1985

How to Cook Husbands
Elizabeth Strong
Worthington

*New York: Dodge Publishing
Co., 1899*
and:
**The Gentle Art of
Cooking Wives**
*New York: Dodge Publishing
Co., c.1900*

**How to Survive Snack
Attacks Naturally**
Shari and Judi Zucker
*Santa Barbara, Ca.:
Woodbridge Press Publishing
Co., 1979*

TRAVELLERS' TALES

Kinki Tourists' Guide
Anon.
n.p., c.1960
'The name Kinki itself
suggests a rich cultural and
religious heritage...' And we
are told that Kinki woman
no longer walks a respectful
distance behind the man
any more. She's right up
beside him...In fact, 'Kinki
Women Make World's
Best Wives'.

Unprotected Females in Norway; or, The Pleasantest Way of Travelling There
Anon. (Emily or Helen Lowe?)
G. Routledge and Co., 1857
and:
Unprotected Females in Sicily, Calabria, and on the Top of Mount Aetna
Routledge, Warne and Co., 1859

Weymouth, the English Naples
Anon.
Middlesbrough: Hood and Co., 1910
'Go to Weymouth. There you will find pure air, pure water, warm sunshine, bright sea, sweet sloping pebbly beaches, firm fine sands, good bathing, boating, yachting, cycling, golfing, etc. The distance from London is 142½ miles, and the journey takes a few minutes over three hours.' Any suggestion of similarity with Naples is purely ridiculous.

Thinking Black. 22 Years Without a Break in the Long Grass of Central Africa
D. Crawford
Morgan and Scott, 2nd edition, 1913

Malaya Upside Down
Kee-Onn Chin
Singapore: Jitts and Co., 1946

Life and Laughter 'midst the Cannibals
Clifford Whiteley Collinson
Hurst and Blackett, 1926

Relates the hilarious story of
a sailor visiting the Solomon
Islands who avoided being
eaten by cannibals but whose
false teeth fell overboard; in
attempting to retrieve them,
he was eaten alive by a shark.

**Recollections of Squatting
in Victoria**
Edward Micklethwaite Curr
*Melbourne: George Robertson,
1883*

Hacking Through Belgium
Edmund Dane
Hodder and Stoughton, 1914
Dane was also the author of
**Trench Warfare: The
Effects of Spade-Power in
Modern Battles**
United Newspapers, 1915

**Gardening in Egypt: a
Handbook for Gardening
in Lower Egypt**
Walter Draper
Upcott Gill, 1895
'So far as I am aware,
no book on Egyptian
gardening has yet been
published in English…'

Astray in the Forest
Edward Sylvester Ellis
Cassell and Co., 1898

**Through Mashonaland
with Pick and Pen**
Sir James Percy Fitzpatrick
*Johannesburg: The Argus Co.,
1892*

**To Lake Tanganyika in a
Bath Chair**
Annie Boyle Hore
Sampson, Low and Co., 1886

**A Wizard's Wanderings
from China to Peru**
John Watkins Holden
Dean and Sons, 1886

Idle Days in Patagonia
William Henry Hudson
Chapman and Hall, 1893
By a remarkable
coincidence, *another*
William Henry Hudson
was the author of *Idle Hours
in a Library* (San Francisco,
Ca.: W. Doxey, 1897).

The Avalanche Atlas
International Commission
on Snow and Ice of the
International Association of
Hydrological Sciences
(Natural Hazards)
Paris: UNESCO, 1981

Gay Bulgaria
Stowers Johnson
Robert Hale, 1964

Here and There in Yucatan
Alice Le Plongeon
New York: J. W. Bouton, 1886

**In Dwarf Land and
Cannibal Country**
Albert Bushnell Lloyd
T. Fisher Unwin, 1899

**On Sledge and Horseback
to Outcast Siberian Lepers**
Kate Marsden
The Record Press, 1892
With immense
determination, Kate
Marsden risks her life and
health, fights off bears and
wolves, and braves all
manner of hardship during
a 2,000-mile ride across

Russia's icy wastes. Her
mission is apparently
rewarded, as almost a third
of the book consists of
letters from prominent
personages thanking her
and offering aid for her
charitable work. The effect
is slightly diminished by a
range of advertisements for
Dr Jaeger's Sanitary
Woollen System Company
Ltd (who supplied Kate
Marsden with her winter
underwear), Wansborough's
Nipple Shields and the
Earlswood Asylum for
Idiots and Imbeciles.

The Little I Saw of Cuba
Burr McIntosh
F. Tennyson Neely, 1899

Hearts Aglow: Stories of Lepers by the Inland Sea
Honami Nagata (translated by Lois Johnson Erickson)
New York: American Mission to Lepers, 1939

Voyage Up the Amazon and the Lion Smacked His Head Off
Sydney Primost
Macmillan, 1957

Nipponology Without Apology. A publication to further trade relations and goodwill between Great Britain and Japan
W. V. Simmons-Lynn
n.p., 1934–35
This book was published at a time when the principal exports from Britain to Japan included: 'tools, scientific instruments, electrical goods, machinery, cars, cycles' and the principal imports into

Britain from Japan were led by 'tinned salmon, crab, mandarin oranges and pineapples'.

The Far East Comes Nearer
Hessell Tiltman
Jarrolds, 1936

Plowing the Arctic
G. J. Tranter
Hodder and Stoughton, 1944

A Girl's Ride in Iceland
Ethel Brilliana Tweedie
Griffith, Farran and Co., 1889
With an appendix, 'What is a geyser?' by G. Harley. The author also wrote:
Through Finland in Carts
A. and C. Black, 1897

Yofuku; or, Japan in Trousers
Sherard Vines
Wishart and Co., 1931

Versailles: The View from Sweden
Elaine Evans Dee and Guy Walton
New York: Cooper-Hewitt Museum, 1988

Downhill Walking Switzerland
Richard and Linda Williams
Tulsa, Okla.: Old World Travel, 1988
'The newest book on the alternative to uphill walking …' (Publisher's description)

ON YOUR BIKE

Across Asia on a Bicycle
Thomas Gaskell Allen and William Lewis Sachtleben
New York: Century Co., 1894

I Cycled into the Arctic Circle
James Duthie
Aberdeen: Northern Publishers, 1957

Across Siberia on a Bicycle
Robert L. Jefferson
Cycle Press, 1896
Mr Jefferson also went:
Awheel to Moscow and Back
Sampson Low, 1895

and:
To Constantinople on a Bicycle
Cycle Press, 1895

Round the World on a Wheel
John Foster Fraser
Methuen, 1904

140 Quiet Wind Assisted Cycle Routes Between BR Stations
Richard N. Hutchins
Bedford: The Author, 1995

WARNING! Cycling may damage your health:

Cycling as a Cause of Heart Disease
George Arieh Herschell
Baillière, 1896

The Bicycle as a Factor in Genito-urinary Diseases, Prostatitis, Prostatorrhea or Prostatic Catarrh
H. Kane
Watchung, NJ: Albert Saifer Publisher, 1983

12

FANTASTIC FICTION

Novel novels

When Woman Reigns
August Anson
*Oxford: Pen-In-Hand
Publishing Co., 1938*
'A startling forecast of a
pacifist world with Woman
as the Master Sex. A young
Scotch professor of Mental
Science projected into the
third millennium falls
desperately in love with the
young and beautiful
'Princess of Luluana'. He
hears what has happened
since the last World War of
1940.' The dustwrapper
depicts a decidedly non-
pacific amazon in riding
boots, jodhpurs, jacket and
tie, whipping the world
into shape.

A Romance of Bureaucracy
'A–B'
*Allahabad: A. H. Wheeler and
Co., 1893*

Hugging to Music; or, The Waltz to the Grave. A Sketch from Life
'An American Observer'
M. J. Darg; New York: University Publishing Co., 1889; illustrated edition 1890
A moralistic tale featuring Joe Jungle, the Wayback Infidel.

The Nighty Story Book
Anon.
Little Folks' Picture Books, 1910

Assassination of Kennedy Considered as a Downhill Motor Race
J. G. Ballard
Brighton: Unicorn Bookshop, n.d.
and:
Why I Want to Fuck Ronald Reagan
Brighton: Unicorn Bookshop, 1968
Two early works by J. G. Ballard written during a period when the author's political beliefs were at the crossroads.

A Queer Affair
Guy Newell Boothby
F. V. White, 1903

Riggermortis
Frank Bruno
Robert Hale, 1966
Remarkably, this boxing novel is by an Australian ex-hobo-turned-journalist, and not by the British heavyweight champion, who was aged just five at the time of its publication. Mr Bruno the novelist is described as writing 'hard-knuckled pages blazing with biff and stingo...'

We All Killed Grandma
Fredric Brown
T. V. Boardman, 1954
'From the very topmost
drawer of Fredric Brown's
writing table.'

What Will He Do With It?
Edward George Earle
Lytton Bulwer-Lytton
*Edinburgh: William
Blackwood, 1859*
He takes four thick volumes
to answer the question.

Tosser, Gunman
Frank Carr
Ward Lock and Co., 1939
"Gee! If it ain't Tosser
Smith. What are you doin'
in this neck of the country?'
The cook stiffened as
through his brain flashed
the recollection of his recent
attitude towards his visitor.
His mouth became
curiously dry. Tosser Smith,
gunman, killer, outlaw.
He'd heard tell that Tosser
had killed more men than
any other gunman known to
the country.

Betty's fingers gripped her
quirt tightly… she, too, had
heard of Tosser Smith…'
Carr was also the author of
Two-Gun Lefty (1940) and
Kid Sin, Killer (1941).

Not Like Other Girls
Rosa Carey
Bentley, 1885

The Toff Goes Gay
John Creasey
Evans Brothers, 1951
One of The Toff's stranger
adventures.

The Girl from the Big Horn Country
Mary Ellen Chase
George G. Harrap, 1937
A fictionalized account of the little girl who caused the celebrated battle in this elevated part of the world.

The Fangs of Suet Pudding
Adams Farr
Gerald G. Swan, 1944
'In the heart of France, May 1940... Loreley Vance is suddenly awakened from her sleep by the entry into her room of, so she thought, a burglar. It may be that because he happened to be English, handsome, young and appealing, that she allowed him to hide under her bed, but whatever the reason it began the series of strange and startling events that brought her into the orbit of "Suet Pudding Face" Carl Vipoering, the master Nazi Spy, whose tentacles had spread over a small band of English folk who dared to oppose his

machinations.' (Publisher's description)

'…But Suet Pudding's fat, sunken-eyed egotism was not yet satisfied. If he had a whip I knew he would have cracked it. Instead he clicked his heels smartly to attention. And, for the first time that night, I smelt the stench of crushed violets…'

Fanny at School
Frances Dana Gage
Buffalo, NY: Breed, Butler and Co., 1866

Gay Cottage
Glance Gaylord
(pseudonym of Ives Warren Bradley)
Boston, Mass.: American Tract Society, 1866

The Green Blot
Sinclair Gluck
Mills and Boon, 1927

The Sauciest Boy in the Service. A Story of Pluck and Perseverance.
W. Gordon-Stables
Ward, Lock and Co., 1905

Man-Crazy Nurse
Peggy Graddis
Pyramid Books, 1967

The City of Lost Women
'Griff'
Modern Fiction, n.d.
'Auction of Souls at the Point of a Rod… A stark mystery that makes other stories seem flat and unconvincing by comparison.'

Dildo Kay
Nelson Hayes
Boston, Mass.: Houghton Mifflin, 1940

The Shunned Vicar of the Gilliflowers
Frederick William von Herbert
Andrew Melrose, 1914
In which the author useth the style of the Holy Scriptures to set forth how the Vicar of the Gilliflowers quarrelled with the judge of the village and eke with the people thereof, and could by no manner of means make peace again. After much

travail, wailing and gnashing of teeth all round, the Vicar departeth from this world and the people take possession of his church with much noise and merriment, saying one to another in their coarse language, 'It's a jolly good thing the old crackpot's gone at last'.

Mated with a Clown
Lady Constance Howard
F. V. White, 1884

Groping
Naomi Ellington Jacob
Hutchinson, 1933
Although the author is perhaps better known for her earlier novel *Roots* (Hutchinson, 1931), *Groping* has been unjustly dismissed. It tells the story of Marcus Stern's struggle against adversity and his final victory.
'It is a curious and intimate novel; a small canvas painted with a wealth of personal detail.'

They Die With Their Boots Clean
Gerald Kersh
Heinemann, 1942
Dedicated by the author to the friends 'I got to know and love' in the Coldstream Guards: 'I think that they represent all that is finest in army life'. Undoubtedly, anyone reading even a small section of the prologue will realize just how effectively Kersh has portrayed their qualities:
'A man gets knifed. A throat gets slit. A bomb goes off. The Wogs are out for blood!... As Sergeant Nelson talks his right eye blinks in the smoke of his cigarette. Pensively pursing his lips, he takes his left eye out, polishes it against the bosom of his battle-blouse, and puts it back again. "Is it in straight, Dusty?"'

Stanton's Pulls It Off
Sylvia Little
Stanmore Press, 1948

The Ups and Downs of Lady Di
Annette M. Lyster
National Society's Depository, 1907

Lady Diana makes at least two further appearances in print, notably:
The Disappearance of Lady Diana
Robert Machray
Everett and Co., 1909
and
The Hunt for Pshaw! An Amusingly Idle Satire

Lady Diana
Glasgow: Scottish National Press, 1925

Gay Agony
Harold Manhood
Cape, 1930
Manhood was also the author of *Nightseed* (Jonathan Cape).

How Nell Scored
Bessie Marchant
T. Nelson and Sons, 1929
and:
Lesbia's Little Blunder
Frederick Warne, 1934
A pair of ripping schoolgirl yarns.

The Red Velvet Goat
Josephina Niggli
French, 1939

Mated From the Morgue
John Augustus O'Shea
Spencer Blackett, 1889
Featuring French Legionnaire O'Hara and his friend O'Hoolohan in Paris before the revolution of 1870 '...had wiped out the

FANTASTIC FICTION **163**

legend of the Empire as with a bloody sponge' – and without a hint of necrophilia.

The Romance of a Dull Life
Mrs A. J. Penny
Longman, Green, 1861

Kinky Finds the Clue
Michael Poole (pseudonym of Reginald Heber Poole)
George Newnes, 1948
Bill Quentin vanishes, and Hudson Mott (a celebrated journalist) is called in, aided by his friend Ken Kinsmith, 'otherwise Kinky, who was "something to do" with Scotland Yard. Kinky soon finds there's more to the affair than a missing schoolboy…'

Eight Years of His Life a Blank. The Story of Pioneer Days in South Dakota. A Novel
L. J. Ross
Waterton, S. Dak.: W. R. Lambert, c.1915

Little Loo
William Clark Russell
Sampson, Low, 1883

Tombstones Are Free to Quitters
Ben Sarto
Modern Fiction Ltd, n.d.
The psychology of Sarto is to be brutal: ' "I guess that guy got too much neck," Bigfella said. "But I reckon I twist it okay." '

Our Lady of the Potatoes
Duncan Sprott
Faber and Faber, 1995

Every Inch a Sailor
William Gordon Stables
Nelson, 1897
The right publisher for this measured tome.

Backwards to Lake Como
Loftus Wigram
Peter Davies, 1938

My Poor Dick
1888
He Went for a Soldier
1890

A Gay Little Woman
1897
Beautiful Jim
1900
The Man I Loved
1901
Magnificent Young Man
1902
Dick the Faithful
1905

A selection from the oeuvre of John Strange Winter (the pseudonym of Henrietta Vaughan Stannard), all published by F. V. White. As a woman writer masquerading as a man, she was, in the words of another of her titles, 'Only Human'.

13

AGAINST ALL ODDS

Titles to make the heart sink

Although some of these are no doubt excellent books, they have been given titles that scarcely inspire a potential reader to open the cover, let alone buy them – titles that are incongruous, just plain dull, or guaranteed cures for insomnia.

Jokes Cracked by Lord Aberdeen

Lord Aberdeen (John Campbell Gordon)
Dundee: Valentine, 1929
'In the realm of Wit and Humour, Lord Aberdeen is a name to conjure with. All the kindly geniality of the North comes out in his rich repertoire of stories, and here the Publishers have pleasure in introducing to a wider public a few Gems from his collection.'
Companion volumes in the

JOKES CRACKED BY
LORD ABERDEEN

same tartan-bound series include *Stories Told by Sir James Taggart* (1926), *The Aberdeen Jew* by 'Allan Junior' (1927) and *Hoots!* by John Joy Bell (1929).

My Tablecloths
Ethel Brilliana Tweedie
Hutchinson, 1916

Cameos of Vegetarian Literature
Anon.
Ideal Publishing Union, 1898

1587. A Year of No Importance
Anon.
Calcutta: n.p., n.d.

If; A Nightmare in the Conditional Mood
Anon. ('By the Authors of *Wisdom While You Wait*, *Hustled History*, etc.' – i.e. Charles Larcom Graves and Edward Verall Lucas)
I. Pitman and Sons, 1908

Modern Filing and How to File
Anon.
Rochester, NY: Yawman and Erbe Manufacturing, 3rd edition, 1920

New Teeth for Old Jaws: Bookselling Spiritualised
Anon.
Cole, 1826

The Romance of Tea
Anon.
English and Scottish Joint Co-operative Wholesale Society, 1934

Thoroughly Criticize the 'Gang of Four' and Bring About a New Upsurge in the Movement to Build Tachai-Type Counties Throughout the Country
Anon.
Beijing: Guoji Shudian, 1979

Bold Musings; being an attempt to create fundamental changes in public opinion and to help to emancipate thought

from the thraldom of foolish time honoured tyrant customs; – written, out compliment to the subject, in lines of ten syllables, and in plain language. With an appendix of choice quotations.

Anon.

Printed not Published, 1870–71

'This book has been printed by foreigners to the English language, on the Continent of Europe, and hence some errors of the press which are partly due, however, to my failing eyesight at reading distance... If this book ever becomes public, the author will not feel bound to answer any critics whom he may believe to be sufficiently answered by the authorities quoted by him or by his own logic.'

Not Worth Reading

Sir George Compton Archibald Arthur

Hutchinson and Co., 1914

How to Attain Success Through the Strength of Vibration of Numbers

Sarah Joanna Balliett (ed.)

Atlantic City, NJ: The Author, 9th edition, 1928

Songs of a Chartered Accountant

Arthur Bennett

Gee and Co., 1930

The Joy of Cataloguing

Sanford Berman

Phoenix, Ariz.: The Oryx Press, 1981

'Twixt Twelve and Twenty. Pat Talks to Teenagers

Pat Boone

Englewood Cliffs, NJ: Prentice-Hall, 1958

A Frog's Blimp

Shinta Cho

Tokyo: Kosei Publishing Co., 1981

Decimalism or Progressive Selection. Aristocracy and Democracy transcribed in a fantasia of Common

Sense. Offered seriously to those who when the wind is blowing southerly know a hawk from a handscrew
By a Citizen of No Importance
Boston, Mass.: Richard G. Badger, The Gorham Press, 1928
A new system of democracy to fight the 'Snob-Mob Complex'. Given a nation of 100,000,000, the population would be 'decimalized' into units of 10 people, who would elect 10 million First Grade Selectors, 1 million Second Grade, 100,000 Councilmen, 10,000 supervisors, 1,000 Assemblymen, 100 Congressmen, 10 Federal Senators, and one President.

The Dream Palaces of Birmingham
Chris and Rosemary Clegg
Birmingham: The Authors, 1983

The Diary of an Organist's Apprentice at Durham Cathedral (1871–1875)
Thomas Henry Collinson (ed. F. Collinson)
Aberdeen: Aberdeen University Press, 1982

The Rubaiyat of a Scotch Terrier
Sewell Collins
Grant Richards, 1926

To Know a Fly
Vincent Gaston Dethier
San Francisco, Ca.: Holden-Day, 1962

An Irishman's Difficulties with the Dutch Language

'Cuey-na-Gael' (pseudonym of the Rev. Dr John Irwin Brown)
Rotterdam: J. M. Bredee, 1908

Such was the success (it went through eight editions between 1908 and 1928) of this genial guide that a further volume was published, entitled *O'Neill's Further Adventures in Holland.*

A Selected Bibliography of Snoring or Sonorous Breathing

Marcus H. Boulware
Nashville, Tenn.: Sonorous Breathing Research Project, Tennessee State A and I University, 1967

Blessed Be Drudgery

William Gannet Channing
n.p., 1897
'With a preface by the Countess of Aberdeen.'

Flooty Hobbs and the Jiggling, Jolly Gollywobber

J. W. Dixon and Jem Sullivan
Miami, Fla.: Hefty Publishing Co., 1991

Sweet Sleep. A Course of Reading Intended to Promote That Delightful Enjoyment

Charles J. Dunphie
Tinsley Brothers, 1879
By the author of the only slightly more lively *Wildfire* (n.p., 1876), it contains chapters guaranteed to beat

counting sheep, including:
The Polite Arts of
    Yawning and Snoring
The Misery of Having
    One's Hair Cut
The Pleasures of Poverty
On the Unimportance of
    Everything
The Delights of the
    English Climate
Pancakes

The Romance of Cement

Edison Portland Cement
Company
*Providence: Livermore and
Knight Co., 1926*

War in Dollyland
(A Book and a Game)

Harry Golding
Ward, Lock and Co., 1915
Tells the colourful story of
the battle between the Flat
Heads and the Wooden
Heads.

'The war fever is catch-
ing – awfully catching', and
it is a war in which no holds
are barred.

'The spy was led out at
dawn… He died as a brave
man should', as can be seen
in the brilliantly realistic
tableau below.

**Ralph Edwards of
Lonesome Lake
Fogswamp
Ruffles On My
Longjohns**
Isabel K. Edwards
Saaichton: Hancock House
The final volume of this
trilogy was published in
1980.

**Wigan Free Public
Library: Its Rise and
Progress**
Henry Tennyson Folkard
*Wigan: 'Privately printed',
1901*

Splay Feet Splashings
'Goosestep'
Leadenhall Press, 1891

**Twinkle, Twankle and
Twunkle**
Arthur R. Griffith
Glasgow: Kym, 1945
Illustrated with
photographs of model elves.

**Just Ordinary, But…
An Autobiography**
Joseph Halliday

*Waltham Abbey: The Author,
1959*

**Hippy. In Memoriam.
The Story of a Dog**
Sir Nevile Meyrick
Henderson
Hodder and Stoughton, 1942
In a year when most people
had weightier matters on
their minds, Sir Nevile
Henderson (late British
Ambassador to the court of
Herr Hitler) chose to publish
a biography of his dachs-
bracke, illustrated with sever-
al fascinating photographs,
including 'Sir Nevile
Henderson with Hippy at a
Royal Shoot at the summer
residence of the late King
Alexander of Yugoslavia'.

The Fourth Dimension
C. Howard Hinton
*Swan Sonnenschein and Co.,
1904*
Impenetrable 'Rot', as a previous explorer of the 'higher
dimensionality of space' has
scribbled on the title page of
the authors' copy.

The Adventures of Chit Chat the Talking Mirror Dinghy
Carole Hughes
Freshwater: Coach House Publications, 1995

Amor
Anai Imaya
Counter-Point Publications, 1984
'A small book of forty poems, but what poems! Every single one of them a masterpiece.' (Emmanuel Gounalakis, Publisher)
'In your Armenian landscape I want to explore every
  crevice in Yerevan
Slowly climb the swollen
  Mount of Ararat
And my arid mouth will
  drink from
The lubricious waters of
  the gushing Arax.'

Working with British Rail
Hugh Jenkins
Batsford, 1984

Jonathan, the Seagull Who Learned to Talk
Foster Macy Johnson
Meriden, Conn.: Bayberry Hill Press, 1963
Predates Richard Bach's *Jonathan Livingston Seagull* by 10 years.

Muddling Toward Frugality
Warren A. Johnson
San Francisco, Ca.: Sierra Club, 1978

A Letter to the Man Who Killed My Dog
Richard Joseph
New York: Frederick Fell, 1956

Freedom Must Not Stink
Dosabhia Framji Karaka
Bombay: Kutub, 1947

New Mexicans I Knew: Memoirs, 1892–1969
William A. Keleher
Albuquerque, NM: University of New Mexico Press, 1983

I Was Hitler's Maid
Pauline Kohler
Long, 1940

The Lull Before Dorking
Sir Baldwyn Leighton
R. Bentley and Son, 1871

Follow Your Broken Nose
Honor McKay
Lutterworth, 1950

**Whereon the Wild Thyme
Blows: Some Memoirs of
Service with the Hong
Kong Bank**
J. F. Marshall
Token, 1986

Dumps; a Plain Girl
Elizabeth Thomasina
Meade
W. and R. Chambers, 1905

I Was a Kamikaze
Ryuji Nagatsuka
Abelard-Schuman, 1973

250 Times I Saw a Play
Keith Odo Newman
Oxford: Pelagos Press, 1944
In the course of the book,

the author fails to mention
what the play was, who
wrote it, where it was performed, and who acted in it.

**Snoring as a Fine Art, and
Twelve Other Essays**
Albert Jay Nock
*Freeport, NY: Books for
Libraries Press, 1958*

**Romance of the Gas
Industry**
Oscar E. Norman
*Chicago, Ill.: A. C. McClurg
and Co., 1922*

The 12C Bus: From Theory to Practice
Dominique Paret
Wiley, 1997

The Wit of Prince Philip
HRH Prince Philip
Leslie Frewin, 1965

A Nostalgia for Camels
Christopher Rand
Boston, Mass.: Atlantic Monthly Press and Little, Brown and Co., 1957
By acquiring the Scarsdale Public Library's discarded copy of this book, the authors have removed it from circulation and thereby deprived the local rummage sales of their most regularly donated item.

The Mother of Goethe
Margaret Reeks
John Lane, 1911

The English. Are They Human?
Dr G. J. Rennier
Williams and Norgate, 1931

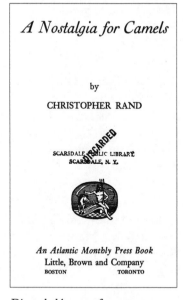

Discarded but not forgotten...

The Elusive Art of Accounting
Howard Ross
New York: The Ronald Press, 1966

The Meaning of Unintelligibility in Modern Art
Edward Francis Rothschild
Chicago, Ill.: University of Chicago Press, 1934

It's a Wog's Life. By Golly
Sidney Samuel Theodore
Rowe
*Hanley: Privately printed for
the author by Webberley Ltd.,
1966*
Reminiscences of a 'Hindu
Aryan's' education at
'Foxhouse', Calcutta, 'in the
best British Public School
Tradition'. The chapter
headings include:
Let sleeping wogs lie
Watch wog
Barking wogs
Give a wog a bone
Cats and wogs
Mad wogs and Englishmen
In the wog house

Banana Circus
Henry Rox and Margaret
Fish
*Hammond Hammond Co.,
1943*
An entire circus troupe
of bananas dressed as
tightrope-walkers, clowns,
jugglers, lion-tamers and
banana animals. A
surprising production,
considering its date of
publication, when bananas
were virtually unavailable in
the UK.

Heroic Virgins
Alfonso P. Santos
*Quezon City, Philippines:
National Book Store, 1977*

The Musings of a Martian
'Sea-Pup'
*Heath Cranton Ltd., Fleet
Street, 1920*
'Of literary talent I have none
(but) I can claim to have had
an almost unique experience
of naval, military and
Ministry of Pensions
hospitals... When I entered
hospital I was a boy... I have
emerged from hospital life to
find a new manhood...' Short
essays by an alienated man
constantly on the sick list.

A Holiday with a Hegelian
Francis Sedlak
A. C. Fifield, 1911
Opens with a chapter on
'What is Thought?' The
author does not seem to have
had much of a holiday.

Golden Quotations of Our First Lady
Julio F. Silvero
Caloocan City, Philippines: National Book [Boot?] Store, 1978
Three-hundred quotations from Imelda Marcos (such as 'Where's the nearest shoe shop?').

Curiosities of Impecuniosity
H. G. Somerville
Richard Bentley and Son, 1896

Chancho. A Boy and His Pig in Peru
Sutherland Stark
Redhill: Wells Gardner, Darton and Co., 1947

What's Wrong with England? A Timely exposure and scathing indictment of amazing British foibles, ludicrous conventions, archaic laws, inefficiency, apathy, sloth, smug complacency, sickly sentiment, hypocrisy, humbug, chaos and confusion responsible for Britain's degeneracy! Pepper Papers seasoned with Sage, Salt and Vinegar. A faithful record of conditions prevailing in post-war Britain.
A. Leonard Summers
Robert Hayes, 1928

The Bright Side of Prison Life
Captain S. A. Swiggett
Baltimore, Md.: Fleet, McGinley and Co., 1897

Five Years' Hell in a Country Parish
Rev. Edward Fitzgerald Synott
Stanley Paul and Co., 1920
Poor old Synott, the Rector of Rusper, accepted the living of Rusper in East Sussex thinking it would be a doddle: '...a sheltered rectory, over which the golden honeysuckle climbed. My flock were to be a few good-hearted rustics, who would greet

their rector with a doff of the hat or an old-fashioned curtsey.' However... 'I feel I must describe in all their terrible realism some of the agonising experiences through which I have passed'. In short, the good people of Rusper did not take too kindly to a vicar more used to working with Barnardo children in London's East End, rather than tittle-tattling, wealthy country grandees. They tried to remove him by gossip and slander, and Synott ended up in a Consistory Court – only to be acquitted of charges of impropriety.

(A Lineal Descendant of the Hereditary Standard or Ensign Bearers of Normandy and England from the Year 911 AD to 1309 AD When the Last of the Main Line Died Childless:) The History of the 'Thorn Tree and Bush' from the Earliest to the Present Time in which Is Clearly and Plainly Shewn the Descent of Her Most Gracious Majesty and Her Anglo-Saxon People from the Half-tribe of Ephraim and Possibly from the Half-tribe of Maaseh, and Consequently Her Right and Title to Possess, at the Proper Moment, for Herself and for Them, a Share, or Shares of the Desolate Cities and Places in the Land of Their Forefathers
M. D. Theta
(pseudonym of William Thorn)
Printed for Private Circulation, 1862
The copy shown to the authors was completely unopened.

Man: The Prodigy and Freak of Nature; or, An Animal Run to Brain
J. C. 'Keridon' Thomas
Watts and Co., 1907

Along Wit's Trail: The Humor and Wisdom of Ronald Reagan
L. William Troxler
New York: Owl Books, 1984
'He has been called the funniest president since Lincoln.' (Publisher's catalogue)

Averroes' Tahafut Al-Tahafut. The Incoherence of the Incoherence
Simon Van Den Bergh (translation from the Arabic)
Luzac and Co., 1954

Passport to Survival: No.1 How to Lose £30,000,000
Elijah Wilkes
Routledge and Kegan Paul, 1955
Described as 'A series of political pamphlets which analyse the evils from which our society is suffering today'. Apparently this was the only title in the series published, as it lost money.

The Skeleton Edition of the Book of Comprehension No.1 'The Preparation X.13: The Rose of Colour Reference for Technical, Kindergarten and Nature Teachers'
Frederick J. Wilson
The Comprehensional Association, n.d.
An incomprehensible book by the editor of *The Comprehensionist*.

Baboo English as 'Tis Writ. Being Curiosities of Indian Journalism
Arnold Wright
T. Fisher Unwin, 1891
'A British-born seaman, with the appropriate name of Butcher belonging to the B. S. Nebo, last Saturday evening in Bowbazar Street, made a sport of an elderly native by striking him on the head. The effect of the joke was instantaneous. The poor Indian fell down insensible and died in hospital.'

14

GOOD BOOKS

Unorthodox religious works

**The Love Letters of a
Portuguese Nun**
Marianna Alcoforado
Cassell, 1890

**Chewable Vitamin 'C' for
the Spirit**
Anon.
*Lancaster, Pa.: Starburst
Publishers, 1996*

**The Pious Christian's
Daily Preparation for
Death and Eternity...
For The Use of Persons
in Lingering Sickness
or Under Sorrow and
Affliction**
Anon.
SPCK, 1852
A laugh on every page...

The Joy of the Upright Man
J. B.
n.p., 1619

**From Cleopatra to Christ.
Arguing that the Former
was the Latter's Mother**
A. J. Bethell
The Author, 1921 (4 vols)
Unpublished typescript in
the British Library.

Rogues of the Bible
James Macdougall Black
*New York: Harper and Bros.,
1930*

**My Invisible Friend
Explains the Bible**
J. G. Bogusz
*Boston, Mass.: Branden Press,
1971*

Becoming a Sensuous Catechist
Therese Boucher
Mystic, Conn.: Twenty-Third Publications, 1984

So Your Wife Came Home Speaking in Tongues! So Did Mine!
Robert Branch
Old Tappan, NJ: Revel, 1973

Hieroglyphic Bibles. Their Origin and History
William Alexander Clouston
Glasgow: D. Bryce and Son, 1894

Lesbian Nuns: Breaking Silence
Rosemary Curb and Nancy Manahan
Tallahassee, Fla.: Naiad Press, 1985

Cooking With God
Lori David and Robert L. Robb
Hollywood, Ca.: Ermine Publishers, 1978

'Cooking with God is truly a labor of love.' (Former First Lady Rosalyn Carter, quoted in the publisher's catalogue)

God Drives a Flying Saucer. Astounding Biblical revelations that prove the existence of UFO's and explain their spiritual significance to mankind
R. L. Dione
Corgi, 1973

Is God Amoeboid?
John W. Doherty
Ringwood: The Author, 1966

Did the Virgin Mary Live and Die in England?
Victor Dunstan
Cardiff: Megiddo Press, 1985

Spiritual Radio
Ferdinand Herbert Du Vernet
Mountain Lakes, NJ: Society of the Nazarene, 1925

Modern Vampirism. Its Dangers and How to Avoid Them

A. Osborne Eaves
Harrogate: Talisman Publishing Co., 1904
Described as 'a practical guide to those under threat', this invaluable book warns: 'With regard to protecting yourself generally, when rising imagine that a shell is forming at the extremity of the aura. Picture a white mist, ovoid, becoming denser every moment. At night again form this protective shell before going to sleep, and you are not likely to be troubled with Vampires. In walking in the street you can prevent yourself being "tapped" by closing the hands, as the fingers conduct the magnetism freely, and many people lose much in this way, which is lapped up from the fingers by astral entities.'

Was Jesus Insane?

G. W. Foote
Progressive Publishing Co., 1891
'Nearly all the modern founders of Christian sects have been more or less demented' so why not the Son of God? '...the act of riding astraddle on two donkeys would alone demonstrate his insanity'.

Twenty Most Asked Questions About the Amish and Mennonites

Merle and Phyllis Good
'A People's Place Booklet', 1979

Thirty-six Reasons for Believing in Everlasting Punishment

David Ponting Hendy
Marshall Bros., 1887

Demonstration of the Spirit Originally Called Shouting

George W. Henry
Ottawa: Holiness Movement Publishing House, 1908

Mr Henry also brought us:
History of the Jumpers
Waukesha, Wis.: Metropolitan Church Association, 1909
and
Shouting; Genuine and Spurious
Oneida, New York: The Author, 1859

Walled Up Nuns and Nuns Walled In
Lancelot Holland
The Author, 3rd edition, c.1895

Entered at Stationers' Hall.]   [*Third Edition.*

WALLED UP NUNS

AND

NUNS WALLED IN.

BY

W LANCELOT HOLLAND, M.A..

EDINBURGH.

Compiler of the " Bible Hymnal."
Author of " The Beauty of Holiness."
Editor of " Convent Life in the Church of England."
etc., etc.

WITH TWENTY ILLUSTRATIONS.

The Manliness of Christ
Thomas Hughes
Macmillan, 1879

Mathematical Principles of Theology; or, The Existence of God Geometrically Demonstrated
Richard Jack
C. Hawkins, 1745

I Love Idi Amin
Festo Kivengere
Marshall, Morgan and Scott, 1977
In the 'New Life Ventures' series, which promises 'a unique and exciting way to see God working in the lives of Christians everywhere'.

The Boo Hoo Bible: The Neo-American Church Catechism
Art Kleps
San Cristobal, N. Mex.: Toad Books, 1971

Esperança de Israel
Manasseh Ben Israel
Amsterdam: n.p., 1650
Promotes the theory that South American Indians are the lost tribe of Israel.

De Concillatione Spiritum: von der Kuzist sich mit Geistern bekant zu machen
H. A. Matke and G. E. Hamberger
n.p., 1716
The title translates as 'On the conciliation of spirits, or how to get acquainted with ghosts'.

The Magic of Telephone Evangelism
Harold E. Metcalf
Atlanta, Ga.: Southern Union Conference, 1967

Traditional Aspects of Hell
James Mew
Swan Sonnenschein and Co., 1903
Mew was also co-author of *Drinks of the World*

(Leadenhall Press, 1892), and translator of *Grammar of the Congo* (Hodder and Stoughton, 1882).

God's Gym: Divine Male Bodies in the Bible
Stephen D. Moore
Routledge, 1996

Christ with the CID
Ex-Chief Inspector Reginald Morrish
Epworth Press, 1953

Would Christ Belong to a Labor Union? or, Henry Fielding's Dream
Rev. Cortland Myers
New York: Street and Smith, c.1900

The Beatles: a Study in Drugs, Sex and Revolution
David A. Noebel
Tulsa, Okla.: Christian Crusade Publications, 1969
A natural successor to the author's earlier:
Communism, Hypnotism and the Beatles
Tulsa, Okla.: Christian Concorde, 1965
and:
Rhythm, Riots and Revolution; an Analysis of the Communist Use of Music, the Communist Master Music Plan
Tulsa, Okla.: Christian Crusade Publications, 1966

Historic Nuns
Bessie Rayner Parkes
Duckworth, 1898

Masturbation in the American Catholic Church
Michael Stephen Patton
Ann Arbor, Mich.: University Microfilms International, 1984

Wrestlers with Christ
Karl Pfleger (translated by E. I. Watkin)
Sheed and Ward, 1936

The Chemical History of the Six Days of Creation
John Phin
New York: American News Co., 1870
Phin later turned to less weighty subjects, including: *The Preparation and Use of Cements and Glue* (1881) and *Trichinae (Pork Worms or Flesh Worms): How to Detect Them, and How to Avoid Them* (1881), and the *Bicyclist's Handbook* (1896),

The Sacred and the Feminine: Toward a Theology of Housework
Kathryn Allen Rabuzzi
New York: Seabury Press, 1982
'An insightful examination of the theological dimension and ritual aspects of housework as performed within the confines of our traditional male culture.'
(Publisher's catalogue)

Hell: Where Is It?
'Saladin' (pseudonym of W. Stewart Ross)
New edition, W. Stewart and Co., c.1890
'If there be no Hell, what use is there for you (Archbishop of York)? Your sole purpose upon Earth is to keep people out of Hell...if there be no Hell, not only what is the use of you, but what is the use of your Christ?' Another of his pamphlets, *The Bottomless Pit*, was reviewed by the *Brighton Herald*: 'Amid his wild and whirling words one can recognise the qualities of a fine mind and a fervent spirit.'

**Ex-Nuns: a Study of
Emergent Role Passage**
Lucinda F. San Giovanni
*Norwood, NJ: Ablex
Publishing Corporation, 1978*

**Why Jesus Never Wrote
a Book**
William Edwin Robert
Sangster
Epworth Press, 1932

**Electricity and
Christianity**
Crump J. Strickland
*Charlotte, NC: Elizabeth
Publishing, 1938*

**The Normal Production
of Psychic Gloves**
Robin John Tillyard
New York: n.p., 1928

**All for the King's Delight:
A Treatise on Chastity
Principally for Religious
Sisters**
F. Valentine
Burns and Oates, 1958

Pilgrims who Jump
Mrs J. E. Whitby
Pearson's Magazine, 1898
An annual procession in
Echternach, Luxembourg,
'…intended to ameliorate or
cure St. Vitus' dance or
epilepsy' and led by the
'jumping saints'. Mrs
Whitby remarks that
'…the appearance of thou-
sands of persons jumping in
rows under open umbrellas
which rise and fall to the
monotonous tune, and the
terpsichorean efforts of
their owners is, despite
the evident seriousness
of the performers, comic in
the extreme'.

**Dirty Laundry: 100 Days
in a Zen Monastery**
Robert Winson and Miriam
Sagan
*Albuquerque, NM: La
Alameda Press, 1997*

15

PECULIARITIES OF THE PRESS

Publishing curiosities and assorted trivia

AN AWFUL BIND

Auto-destruct bindings:
The notorious B. F. Hardwick of Bradford has been justly described as 'probably the world's worst binder'. He flourished towards the end of the nineteenth century, and certain features of his bindings can be spotted across a crowded bookshop. These include:
1. His use of half pig-skin, heavily tanned, which reduces to powder with handling.
2. Neat trimming of the margins often affecting the text area, for example: a copy of Wordsworth's *White Doe of Rylstone* which Hardwick reduced from quarto to octavo.
3. Rounding of corners further reducing the margins.
4. Highly durable imitation alligator-skin boards.
5. A binder's label that has a pronounced tendency to oxidize and disintegrate.

Black-lace panties:
Grand Opening: A Year in the Life of a Total Wife
Alice Whitman Leeds
Jackson Heights, NY: 1980
A one-off production. Pink satin, trimmed in lace; front cover embellished with black lace panties with gun inserted.

Cigar-box boards:
*The Soverane Herbe: A
History of Tobacco*
W. A. Penn
New York: Dutton, 1901

Cricketiana:
Baxter's Second Innings
Henry Drummond
Hodder and Stoughton, 1892
The authors have seen three
unusual bindings of the
cricket book of Scottish
theologian, Henry
Drummond (1851–97).
Two copies are in striped

cloth in the style of a
Victorian cricket blazer or
a club tie, one with the title
in the form of a blazer
badge, the other resembling
a linen name-tape. The
third is a unique *pièce de
resistance* – bound in off-
white kid to resemble a
miniature cricket pad.

Denim:
How the Other Half Lives
Jacob Auguste Riis
*New York: Charles Scribner's
Sons, 1890*

What the well-dressed cricketing book is wearing this season.

Originally offered for sale bound in denim from a workman's overalls.

Fireproof edition:
Fahrenheit 451
Ray Bradbury
n.p.,1953
Fireproof edition of 200 copies bound in asbestos boards.

Fishskin:
A copy of Isaac Walton's *The Compleat Angler* has been bound in fishskin, tanned by a process invented in Germany during the First World War by Hermann G. Schmid.

Greaseproof paper:
Alexandri Magni
Curtius Rufus
n.p., 1696
A fine example seen by the authors was sympathetically bound in 'full greaseproof marbled lining paper with black Dymo-tape spine label'.

Handkerchief:
The Love Sonnets of a Hoodlum
Wallace Irwin
San Francisco, Ca: Paul Elder, 1901
Mr Irving's 'dulcet vagaries' are clothed in a rather colourful handkerchief.

Human Skin:
Narrative of the Life of James Allen, alias George Walton, alias Jonas Pierce, alias James H. York, alias Burley Grove, the Highwayman, Being His Death-bed Confession to the Warden of the Massachusetts State Prison
James Allen
Boston, Mass.: Harrington and Co., 1837
The Boston Athenaeum has the ultimate in autobi-ography – a copy bound in the author's own skin.
also:
Poetical Works
John Milton
n.p., 1830
The Albert Memorial

Library, Exeter, possesses
a copy bound in the skin
of a murderer, George
Cudmore.

Leopard-skin throughout:
The Jayne Mansfield Story
Barton L. Benes
New York: n.p., 1979

Malodorous edition:
The collection of Captain
Maurice Hamonneau
includes a copy of Adolf
Hitler's *Mein Kampf* bound
in skunk skin.

Map jacket:
Nancy Kennedy
*The Ford Treasury of
Favorite Recipes from
Famous Eating Places*
*New York: Simon and
Schuster, 1950*
'Remove and open up this
jacket. Inside is a beautiful
full-color map of the United
States to decorate your
kitchen or game room.' And
when you have unfolded it,
what could look more

agreeable in your game
room than a heavily-creased
map of America with no
states or towns identified?

Of Human Bandage:
*God's Revenge Against
Murder*
John of Exeter
n.p., 1740
The book features splendid
copperplates of stabbing,
dismembering, garrotting,
etc, and the authors have
been shown a copy rebound
in slightly soiled bandages
by its owner, a gentleman
of Bristol.

Plywood:
Modern Plywood
Anon.
Pitman Publishing Co., n.d.

A rattling good yarn:
Also in the Hamonneau
collection, there is a copy of
Clare Booth Luce's *The
Woman* with a rattlesnake
rattle in the binding to warn
off any reader attempting to
open the book.

Sheets:
Rise and Fall of Carol Banks
Elliott White Spring
n.p., n.d.
Printed on glazed cotton
sheets, bound in blue
bedspread material from the
author's own mill, and
jacketed in little hem-
stitched pillowcases.

**Straw, alfalfa seed and a
Webster's Dictionary
(c.1950):**
*Two Sprout Books: Seed
Thoughts*
Douglas Benbe
New York: 1984
'Alfalfa seeds interspersed
with straw pulp and shred-
ded pages of the dictionary.
This mix then poured into
deckle box or paper mould.
This formed sheets trans-
ferred on to a flat surface
where they were stacked
and allowed to sprout.

Each day the pages were
watered and tended. The
intention is that the pages
of these books open as a
result of the growth of the
sprouts and that the closing
of these books will occur
when they are no longer
watered. As the sprouts
die, each page will begin
to close.

We participate by
watching the process of
their transformation over
time.'

Uniform edition:
In the Hamonneau collec-
tion there is a copy of Erich
Maria Remarque's *All Quiet
on the Western Front* bound
in part of a First World War
uniform.

Wood samples:
The Schildbach collection
contains samples of
different woods made up by
an eighteenth-century zoo-
keeper to look like books.
One side of each volume
opens to reveal samples of
the tree's leaves, flowers,
fruit, seeds and roots.

STRANGE DEDICATIONS; OR, IF YOU CAN'T SAY SOMETHING NICE...

Sahara
Angus Buchanan
John Murray, 1926
'To Ferri n'Gashi, Only a camel, But steel-true and Great of heart.'

Hodgepodge: A Commonplace Book
Joseph Bryan III
New York: Simon and Schuster, 1986
'For my ouaffe, from her ossban' (the writer's Franglais version of 'wife' and 'husband').

An Essay on Silence
Michael Chater
Abbey Mills Press, 1969
A book of blank paper samples, dedicated to '...those who enjoy the sight and feel of good books, but to their sorrow have little time for reading them.'

Did I Do That?
John Clarmont
Lewes: Book Guild, 1987
'To no one in particular.'

Green Memory of Days with Gun and Rod
J. B. Drought
Philip Allan, 1937
'To the best bag I ever made in Ireland – My Wife.'

Alcoolisme et Absinthisme
Maurice Gourmet
Montpellier: Printed by Firmin et Cabirou, 1875
'A la mémoire de mon père.'

Venereal Disease and Its Prevention
Felix Raoul Leblanc
Letchworth: G. W. Browne, 1920
'To my wife this book is affectionately dedicated.'

The Desert Rose
Larry McMurtry
New York: Simon and Schuster, 1985

'For Leslie, for the use of her goat.'
The author also wrote the novel of the Oscar-winning film *Terms of Endearment.*

Bedfordshire, Huntingdon and Peterborough

(Buildings of England series)
Nikolaus Pevsner
Harmondsworth: Penguin Books, 1968
'To the inventor of the iced lolly.'

1,001 Obscure Points

Jacob Schwartz
Bristol: The Chatford House Press, 1931
Dedicated to the bibliographer who insured himself against going mad.

The Other Side of Midnight

Sidney Sheldon
New York: William Morrow, 1974
'To Jorga, who pleasures me greatly.'

Tristram Shandy

Laurence Sterne
York: Ann Ward, 1760
'To be let or sold for fifty guineas.'

Memoirs and Anecdotes of Philip Thicknesse, Late Lieutenant Governor of Land Guard Fort, and, Unfortunately Father to George Touchet, Baron Audley

Philip Thicknesse
Printed for The Author, 1788–91
Celebrated traveller and eccentric Philip Thicknesse abuses his son on the title-page of his *Memoirs*, but his full venom is reserved for the dedicatee who had previously accused Thicknesse of cowardice during a minor military action against Jamaican rebels:

'To James Makittrick, alias Adair, James Makittrick Adair then. Greeting,
As it is to you whose conduct I am obliged, for

The vituperative Philip Thicknesse

the very honourable and respectable names, which appear at the head of the following chapters; and who have kindly enabled me (without expence) to vindicate my character, and to defend my honour against a base defamer, a vindicative libeller, and a scurrilous, indecent, and vulgar scribbler; you are certainly the properest man existing, to address them to...'

Makittrick found the attack entertaining and is included in a supplementary subscribers' list in Volume 2 as a purchaser of 200 copies of the book.

A Bibliography of Books on the Circus in English from 1773 to 1964
Raymond Toole-Scott
Derby: Harpur and Sons, 1964
'In Memory of my Pussy.'

Possessing the Secret of Joy
Alice Walker
New York: Harcourt Brace, 1992
'To the Blameless Vulva.'
Walker is better known as the author of the novel *The Color Purple*, on which the award-winning film was based.

EXERCISES IN MAKING LIFE DIFFICULT

The Greek poet Tryphiodorus wrote an epic poem, *Odyssey*, in twenty-four books, each one leaving out words containing a letter of the Greek alphabet. He started a trend for 'lipograms' – works in which certain letters are deliberately omitted – that has been followed by such writers as Lope de Vega, who produced five novels, each avoiding one vowel and Gregorio Leti, who wrote a book without a single letter 'e'. Among other lipogrammatic books are:

Voyage Autour du Monde Sans la Lettre A
Jacques Etienne Victor Arago
Paris: n.p., 1853
The letter 'a' appeared in the word 'serait' in the first edition; this was edited out in the second. 'A', of course, does appear five times in the title.

La Pièce Sans A
J. R. Ronden
Paris: n.p., 1816
This was performed as a play at the Paris Théâtre des Variétés on 18 December 1816. It somewhat taxed its actors, causing a riot among the audience, who did not allow it to run to its end.

Gadsby
Ernest Vincent Wright
Los Angeles, Ca.: Wetzel Publishing Co., 1939
F. Scott Fitzgerald's finest book, *The Great Gatsby*, had been published in 1925; undaunted, in 1939 Wright took 165 days to write a novel with the not dissimilar title of *Gadsby*. But there the similarity ended, for Wright's book was unique – and it could scarcely have had either 'The' or 'Great' in its title – for in all its 50,000 words there was not one containing the letter 'e'. Wright's achievement was astonishing, since this was a book of nearly 300 pages and 'e' is by far the most common letter in the English language. By taping down the 'e' key on his typewriter to make it impossible to use, and by using substitute words throughout (such as 'said' instead of 'replied'), he succeeded in writing prose that is, remarkably, not

noticeably forced. But the strain was too much for him, and on the day of publication, Wright died. After his death, copies of *Gadsby* were to become highly prized among collectors of rare books, and now change hands for large sums.

Then there are those who have gone to the opposite extreme, writing works where every word begins with the same letter, such as:

Ecologa de Calvis
Hucbaldus
Basle: Jacobus Parcum, 1546
A poem in praise of bald people, consisting exclusively of words beginning with 'c' – and dedicated to Charles the Bald.

Pugna Porcorum
Publius Porcius (pseudonym of Johannes Placentius)
Cologne, 1530
It is written in Latin and all the words begin with the letter 'p'. After several hundred lines like 'Plaudant porcelli, portent per plaustra patronum', this gets rather tedious.

Sunday; or, A Working Girl's Lament
Daisy Fellowes
Monaco: A. Chêne, 1930
The author of *Cats in the Isle of Man* (1929) attempted in this book to introduce a revolutionary concept of poetic dialogue whereby the text is printed in black, red, green or mauve, according to who is speaking. This complex typography was clearly beyond her printer, and the result contains so many mistakes that every one of the 200 limited edition copies has the appearance of a scrapbook into which are pasted odd words and whole stanzas of corrected text.

EDITORS AND PRINTERS BEWARE

Strange Tales from Humlbe [sic] Life. Sold at a reduced price in Scotland only, by the Religious Tract Society, for behoof [sic] of the working classes.
John Ashworth
Manchester: Tubbs and Brook, c.1874

A special edition with a cancel title apparently set by a trainee gravestone cutter with all the traditional accuracy associated with that craft.

Missae ac Missalis Anatomia
n.p., 1561
A 172-page Latin missal with a 15-page errata, blamed by its printer on the devil.

Notes on the History of Redruth
F. Mitchell
n.p., c.1945
A 117-page book with a 17-page corrigenda.

Oliver Twist
Mark Twain
Athens: Harmi-Press, 1963
Attributed to Mark Twain on the cover, but the publishers managed to credit Charles Dickens on the titlepage.

SPELLING AND PUNCTUATION ODDITIES

The Gates of Paradise
Jerzy Andrzejewski
(translated by James
Kirkup)
Weidenfeld and Nicolson,
1962
Although it contains
commas, semi-colons and
some other punctuation, the
first full stop does not
appear until page 158 – the
last page of the book.

The Feminin Monarchi;
or, The Histori of Bees
Charles Butler
Oxford: Printed by William
Turner for The Author, 1634
Written in phonetic spelling
throughout.

A Pickle for the Knowing
Ones; or, Plain Truths in a
Homespun Dress
Timothy Dexter
Salem, Mass.: Printed for The
Author, 1802

No punctuation appeared in
any edition until 1838,
when Dexter added a page
with 13 lines consisting of
rows of commas, colons,
exclamation and question
marks, and full stops, which
he suggested readers may
'peper and solt' throughout
his book 'as they plese'.

The Elements of
Geometry
John Dobson
Cambridge: Cambridge
University Press, 1813 and
1815 (2 vols)
An impenetrable textbook
with almost no punctuation.

The Quick Brown Fox
Richard G. Templeton Jr.
Chicago, Ill.: At the Sign of
the Gargoyle, 1945
Contains thirty-three
sentences, each containing
all twenty-six letters of the
alphabet.

TWO EXCURSIONS INTO THE UNNECESSARY

To the Curious: The Word Scissars [sic] Appears Capable of More Variations in the Spelling than Any Other
Anon.
Enfield: T. T. Barrow, 1829
There are two copies of this broadsheet in the British Library: one lists 240 ways of spelling 'scissars', and the other, by using double letters, has 480. Variants include:
Sisszyrs
Cisors
Scysors
Cyzsyrs

An Historical Curiosity, by a Birmingham Resident. One Hundred and Forty-one Ways of Spelling Birmingham
William Hamper
Charles Whittingham, 1880

ODD VOLUMES

Book of Common Prayer
Engraved and Printed by John Sturt, 1717
The titlepage verso has a portrait of George I composed of the words of the Lord's Prayer, Ten Commandments, 21st Psalm, etc, which are so small that a magnifying glass is necessary to read them. The entire book is printed from silver plates.

The Undead: The Book Sail [sic] Anniversary Catalogue
Orange, Ca.: Book Sail, n.d.
A limited-edition catalogue of science-fiction and fantasy books, each of the 1,400 copies numbered in human blood.

Stripsody
Eugenio Carmi
Houston, Tx.: Kiko Galleries, 1967
The contents include:
BOINGGGG

ZOOM
WAAACH
bang-BUM
VROOP-ROOP

**Books in Bottles. The
Curious in Literature**
William George Clifford
Geoffrey Bles, 1926

**Sun-beams may be
extracted from cucumbers,
but the process is tedious.
An oration, pronounced
on the Fourth of July, 1799.
At the request of the citizens
of New-Haven**
David Daggett
*New-Haven: Thomas Green
and Son, 1799*

David Copperfield
Charles Dickens
*Editions for the Armed Forces,
Inc., c.1944*
Wartime economy edition,
'Condensed… due to
limitations of space, it has
been necessary to eliminate
some of the material
contained in the original edition of this book.'

**Eleven Years a Drunkard,
or, The Life of Thomas
Doner, Having Lost
Both Arms Through
Intemperance, He Wrote
this Book with His Teeth
as a Warning to Others**
Thomas Doner
*Sycamore, Ill.: Arnold Bros.,
1878*

From legless to armless.

The Posthumous Papers of the Pickwick Club
Charles Dickens
Faudel Phillips and Sons, 1893
A title in the Peacock Library which was 'Printed on pale blue tinted paper, especially manufactured for these books, recommended by Professor Von Hoffman of the Berlin School of Oculists, as being specially suited for preserving the eyesight'.

Worth a thousand words...

What Women Know About Men
F. E. Male (believed to be a pseudonym)
Containing 400 pages, all of them completely blank...

Geschichte Ohne Worte
Frans Masereel
Wiesbaden: Insel-Verlag, 1952
'A Story Without Words' – a series of 60 woodcuts tells the highly original story of man meets girl, man has his way with girl, man dumps girl. The only text is an 'afterword' by Herman Hesse.

How to Clean Up on Horses: Confidential Dope
Carol A. Roberts
Chicago, Ill.: H. Fishlove and Co., 1939
Created by cutting a slot in the pages of an ex-US Army publication, into which are mounted a miniature broom and shovel. Amusing the first time.

Bibliotheca Staffordiensis
Rupert Simms
Lichfield: A. C. Lomax, 1894
The claims to be the first
book written by a man with
no hands. At the age of nine,
Simms got entangled with
machinery in a brickyard.
He was given sixpence from
one partner in the firm, and
threepence by another, and
his hands in a bag.

Sixty Sixties
Jacques P. Solari
The Author, 1897
Solari's work contains
sixty verses, each with sixty
words, commemorating the
sixty years of the reign of
Queen Victoria.

**God's Man: A Novel in
Woodcuts**
Lynd Kendall Ward
Cape, 1930
and
Madman's Drum
Lynd Kendall Ward
Cape, 1930
Another novel without
words.

THE LARGEST NUMBER OF EDITIONS OF THE SAME BOOK*

*Other than the Bible.

**The Etymological
Spelling-Book and
Expositor**
Henry Butter
*Simpkin, Marshall,
Hamilton, Kent and Co.*
The first edition appeared
in about 1830. By 1848 it
had reached 111 and by

H. Butter.

1886 no fewer than 442. The 'new and revised' 1897 edition was not numbered but was described as the 'Two Thousand Four Hundred and Thirty-second Thousand' [2,432,000] and there was an edition as recently as 1941; this modestly stated only that 2,700,000 copies had been sold, but did not include an edition number. The frontispiece portrait in the 1897 edition shows Henry Butter, a bewhiskered Victorian with just a hint of a smirk; he was perhaps thinking about his royalty cheque.

WORLD RECORD 'LIMITED EDITION'

The Man from Glengarry, A Tale of The Ottawa
Ralph Connor
New York: Grosset and Dunlap, 1901
'Limited to 50,000 copies.'

WORLD RECORD SIGNED LIMITED EDITION

My Philosophy
Elbert Hubbard
New York: Roycrofters, 1916
Hubbard's most famous work, *A Message to Garcia* (1899), is believed to have sold 40–50 million copies, so he clearly thought in large numbers. Nonetheless, a limited edition of 9,983 copies of *My Philosophy*, every one signed by the author, is verging on the ostentatious. Even more remarkably, Hubbard went down with the *Lusitania* the year before it was published, so how did he sign them? *X-Files* scriptwriters, take note…

'THE FUNNIEST BOOK IN THE WORLD'

Cole's Fun Doctor: The Funniest Book in the World

Edward William Cole
Routledge, 1886

30,000 of this Fun Doctor were sold in one part of Australia in about 18 months, and 20,000 of them retailed in Cole's Book Arcade, Melbourne. Mr Cole, in the public press, offered a bonus of £100 to any one who could prove that it was not the funniest book in the world, or that ever was in the world. No one has yet been able to claim the bonus, for the simple reason that this is beyond all doubt the funniest book ever published.' This extravagant claim is followed by 350 pages of the unfunniest jokes of all time.

Smiling faces, but few laughs.

INCOMPATIBLE COUPLES

**James Maurice Stockford
Careless**
The Canadians: The Story
of a People
New York: Macmillan, 1938
and
**George MacKinnon
Wrong**
Canada. A History of a
Challenge
*Cambridge: Cambridge
University Press, 1959*
Serious students of
Canadian history are still
waiting for Mr Right to
come along.

**Uncertainty of Spiritual
Intercourse**
and
**Certainty of Spiritual
Intercourse**
John Worth Edmonds
*New York: Spiritual Tracts
Nos. 4 and 5, 1858*

Women Without Men
Marise Querlin
Mayflower-Dell, 1965

and
Men Without Women
Ernest Hemingway
*New York: Charles Scribner's
Sons, 1927*

Hitler's Last Year of Power
Leonardo Blake
Andrew Dakers, 1939
and
**The Man Who Made the
Peace: The Story of Neville
Chamberlain**
Stuart Hodgson
Christophers, October 1938

? AND !!!

?
Sir Walter Newman Flower
Cassell, 1925
and
!!!
George Hughes Hepworth
*New York: Harper and Bros.,
1881*
Hepworth was the author of
*Through Armenia on
Horseback* (Isbister and Co.,
1898).

LONGEST PSEUDO-INITIALISM

In London in 1737, J. Roberts published a book by Arthur Ashley Sykes ('The Precentor And Prebendary of Alton Borealis In The Church Of Salisbury'), *An Enquiry into the Meaning of Demoniacks in the New Testament*, under the pseudonym: 'T.P.A.P.O.A.B.I.T.C.O.S.'

POLYSYLLABIC AND UNPRONOUNCEABLE TITLES

Āryasuvikrāntavikrāmipari-prcchāprajñāpāramitānirde-śasārdhadvisāhasrikā-Bhag-avatyāryaprajñāpāramitā
Bearbeitet von Tokumyo Matsumoto
Tokyo: Verlag Heibonsha, 1956

A reproduction of the only surviving manuscript of this Prajnaparamita, making it the longest-known single word in a title.
(97-character word)

Le 'Boschmannschucrut-undkakafresserdeutschkol-ossalkulturdestruktor-kathedralibusundkinden'
M. C. A. Kinneby
Paris: Les Editions Pratiques et Documentaires, 1915
(84-character word)

The Baron Kinkvervankotsdorsprak-ingatchdern. A New Musical Comedy
Miles Peter Andrews
T. Cadell, 1781
(33-character word)

Hepatopancreatoduode-nectomy
F. Hanyu (ed.)
New York: Springer, 1996
(27-character word)

The Tragedy of Chrononhotonthologos
Henry Carey
J. Shuckburgh and L. Gulliver; J. Jackson, c.1734
This title was originally published under the pseudonym 'Benjamin Bounce'. (20-character word)

Logopandecteision; or, An Introduction to the Universal Language
Sir Thomas Urquhart
Giles Calvert and Richard Tomlins, 1653
Only seventeen characters, but the book is divided into six sections with the titles:
Neaudethaumata
Chrestasebeia
Cleronomaporia
Chryscomystes
Neleodicastes
Philoponauxesis

A PECULIAR CHOICE FOR A PSEUDONYM

History of the City of Chicastop for ten years, 1885 to 1895
A Bummer
Chicago.: n.p., 1884 [sic]

A RATHER INAPPROPRIATE OFFICIAL PUBLICATION

First Report of the Standing Advisory Committee on Artificial Limbs
Ministry of Pensions, 1947

CATALOGUE CURIOSITIES

Taken from the British Library Catalogue:

An exotic piece of ephemera
EJACULATIONS

Ejaculations to be used by a woman during the time of her labour.
London, 1853. a card; quarto

An uncommon collection
A collection of seven miniature volumes containing drawings of six beetles, nutcrackers, clay and briar pipes, horse brasses, scissors and candle-snuffers, American wall and shelf clocks and ancient musical instruments. The first drawn by Marie Angel and the remainder by Pamela Fowler. Bound and chained to a miniature wooden lectern which is encased in a cylinder, leather covered and gold-tooled. Executed at Froxfield by Roger Powell and Peter G. Waters in 1959.

Silliest entry
[Poems] [Edinburgh? 1785?] 12mo.
Imperfect; wanting the titlepage and all before page 17, and after page 24. In other words, a small, anonymous fragment, publisher unknown, date and place of publication uncertain, consisting of an odd eight pages from a larger work.

Perplexing cross-references
MUN (GEN OK)
See OK (Mun Gen)

LING (TING)
See TING (Ling)

FOWL DECEIVER
See POOF. The Fowl Deceiver. A Lay of the Inventions Exhibition, etc.
Field and Tuer, 1885

TOP RHYMING TITLES/AUTHORS

Derwas James Chitty
The Desert a City
Oxford: Blackwell, 1966

Auguste Forel
La Question Sexuelle
Paris: G. Steinheil, 1906

Lady Winifred Fortescue
**'There's Rosemary...
There's Rue...'**
*Edinburgh: William
Blackwood and Sons, 1939*

Herbert Gold
Therefore Be Bold
André Deutsch, 1962

Helena Grose
The Flame and the Rose
Collins, 1954

August Kotzebue
The Spaniards in Peru
R. Phillips, 1799

Mrs John Lane
Maria Again
John Lane, 1915

John Henry O'Hara
Appointment in Samarra
Faber and Faber, 1935

George Ryley Scott
**Marriage in the Melting
Pot**
T. Werner Laurie, 1930

Hawley Smart
A False Start
Chapman and Hall, 1887

Samuel West
How to Examine the Chest
J. A. Churchill, 1883

T. H. White
The Ill-Made Knight
*New York: G. P. Putnam's
Sons, 1940*

16

LAST WRITES

Bizarre books on death – and after

The Sunny Side of Bereavement
Rev. Charles E. Cooledge
Boston, Mass.: Richard G. Badger, The Gorham Press, n.d.

Reusing Old Graves
D. Davies and A. Shaw
Shaw and Sons, 1995

The Practical Embalmer
Asa Johnson Dodge
Boston, Mass.: The Author, 1900

A Handbook on Hanging
Charles St Lawrence Duff
Cayme Press, 1928
This grisly book was first published in 1927 by Cayme Press in Great Britain and in 1929 by Hale, Cushman and Flint of Boston. Clearly popular on both sides of the Atlantic, it was revised and reissued (by John Lane) in 1938 and again in 1948. The version published in London by Andrew Melrose in 1954 is described as the 'Definitive Edition'. The 1961 Putnam edition is the 'finally definitive edition'.

Duff (1894–1966) presents himself on the titlepage as 'Barrister-at-Law' and his book is 'Dedicated Respectfully to The Hangmen of England'. He advocates murder trials in the Albert Hall and Wembley Stadium, with the

The overall effect is so over the top that it is hard to believe that it is anything but a clever attack on supporters of capital punishment, especially as Duff's other published works comprise a range of conventional plays and language-teaching aids.

Sex After Death
B. J. Ferrell and Douglas Edward Frey
New York: Ashley Books, c.1983

sale of film rights to trials and executions, the revenue from which, he argues, could enable the Government to reduce Income Tax.

This bizarre compendium concludes with Duff's 'Ready Reckoner for Hangmen', which gives the universally valuable information of height of drop in relation to the victim's weight.

By His Own Hand: A Study of Cricket's Suicides
David Frith
Stanley Paul, 1991
More than eighty examples of cricketers who have killed themselves.

Deathing: An Intelligent Alternative for the Final Moments of Life
Anya Foos-Graber
Reading, Mass.: Addison-Wesley, 1984

Daddy Was an Undertaker
McDill McCown Gassman
New York: Vantage Press,
1952

The Art of Embalming
Thomas Greenhill
The Author, 1705
His mother, Elizabeth
Greenhill is said to have
had thirty-nine children.

Buried Alive
Franz Hartmann
Boston, Mass.: Occult
Publishing Co., 1895

Hanging in Chains
Albert Hartshorne
T. F. Unwin, 1891

Public Performances of the
Dead
George Jacob Holyoake
London Book Store, 1865

Tell Me, Papa: Tell Me
About Funerals
Marvin and Joy Johnson
Brooklyn, NY: Center for
Thanatology Research and
Education, 1980

How I Know That the
Dead Are Alive
Fanny Ruthven Paget
Washington, DC: Plenty
Publishing Co., 1917

Do-it-Yourself Coffins:
For Pets and People
Dale Power
Atglen, Pa.: Schiffer
Publishers, 1997

Death, Dissection and the
Destitute: The Politics
of the Corpse in
Pre-Victorian Britain
Ruth Richardson
Routledge, 1987

Phone Calls
from the Dead
D. Scott Rogo and
Raymond Bayless
Englewood Cliffs, NJ:
Prentice Hall, 1979
One-way conversations
when the line goes dead.

The Liturgy of Opening
the Mouth for Breathing
Mark Smith
Oxford: Griffith Institute,

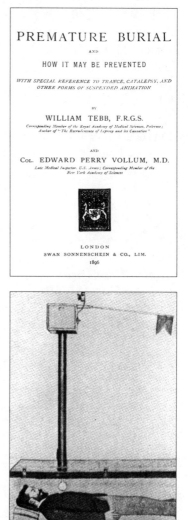

Ashmolean Museum, 1993
On Ancient Egyptian funeral rites.

Premature Burial and How It May Be Prevented

William Tebb and Col. Edward Perry Vollum
Swan Sonnenschein and Co., 1896

The authors conclude that 'no evidence of death is really satisfactory except that which is supplied by putrefaction' and suggest the building of what they describe as 'waiting mortuaries... furnished with every appliance for resuscitation. Only when the fact of death has been unequivocally established by the sign of decomposition' should the body be removed to the cemetery. The seriousness with which the problem was taken can

Here, the 'deceased' squeezes the conveniently placed glass ball to let in air – his life saved for the exceedingly reasonable price of twelve shillings.

perhaps be judged by the ownership stamp of one the copies in the authors' collection: 'Office of the City Coroner, Auckland, 8 July 1907'.

Do the Dead Ever Talk?
Edward Thurston
n.p., 1923

On the Gallows
Violet Van der Elst
The Doge Press, 1937
Van der Elst was also the author of *The Torture Chamber* (The Doge Press, 1934).

Last Chance at Love
Various authors
New York: Pinnacle Books, 1981
In the *Terminal Romances* series.

How to Conduct a One-day Conference on Death Education
Ellen Zinner and Joan McMahon
Brooklyn, NY: Center for Thanatology Research, 1980

ACKNOWLEDGEMENTS

Anon of Nottingham
Caroline Ash
Richard Axe
Michael Baker
Robert Baldock
M. and M. Baldwin
Lionel Barnard
Louis Baum
Robin de Beaumont
Bloomsbury Book Auctions
The Bookdealer
The Bookseller
Nancy Boothe
Simon Brett
Raymond Briggs
British Library Reading Room staff
Stan Brown
A. J. Browning
Karen Bullock
Nigel Burwood
Mark Bryant
Iain Campbell
Mark Campbell
Peter Carter
Pat Cassidy
Philip Chancellor
M. and B. Clapham
Stephen Clarke
Graham Cornish
Countryside Books
John H. Cranwell
James Cummins
Richard Dalby
Paul Davies
Patrick Davis

Rebecca Dearman
The Diagram Group
Paul Dickson
Disley Bookshop
Andrew Duckworth
Roy Eden
John Eggeling
Christopher Eley
Toby English
Len Evans
Sylvia Fenlon
David Fielder
Phil Flowers
Tony Fothergill
Camilla Francombe
Laurie E. Gage
Patrick Gallagher
Joseph L. Gardner
Malcolm Gerratt
David Gillham
Mike and Sue Goldmark
Mike Goodenough
William Goodsir
'The Grandfather from Hell'
Ian Grant
Martin Greif
Liz Groves
William Gummer
E. Hallett
Lionel Halter
Sylvian Hamilton
Gail Harbour
Dave Harris
George G. Harris
John Hart

William Hartston
David Haxby
Chris Heppa
Bernard Higton
Bevis Hillier
Geoff Hinchcliffe
David Holmes
Philip M. Hopper
Horsham Bookshop
D. F. Howard
Philip Howard
Barry Humphries
Mary Hutchinson
Paul Hutchinson
C. Hyland
Chris Irwin
D. Jarvis
Pete Jermy
Christopher Johnson
Annette Jolly
Richard Glyn Jones
Martin Keene
George Kelsale
Keith Kenyon-Thompson
Bryan Kernaghan
Sarah Key
Miles Kington
John Kinnane
Michele Kohler
Eric Korn
Patty Lafferty
Adam Langley
Library Journal
Raymond Lister
George Locke
John A. Lord
Loughborough Bookshop
John Lyle
Ian Lynn
Julian Mackenzie
Maggs Bros.
Vivian T. Maisey
Jo Manning
Anthony Masterton-Smith

Nell McCorry
R. McCutcheon
Rod Mead
A. Micallef Grimaud
S. P. Milanytch
Ian Miller
John Miller
Peter Miller
Brian Mills
Montpelier Books
Michael Moon
C. R. Moore
Charles Mortimer
G. Mosdell
Margaret Nangle
Janet Nassau
New York Public Library
Kent Nielsen
Angus O'Neill
C. J. Phillips
Roy Pitches
Primrose Hill Books
The Printer's Devil
The Provincial Booksellers'
    Fairs Association
Michael Prowse
John Randall
Ann M. Ridler
John D. Roles
Adrian Room
Prof. Robert Rosenthal
Theo Rowland-Entwistle
Ruth Royce
Robert Rubin
Christine A. Ruggere
Matthew Searle
Tony Seaton
Barry Shaw
Brian Shawcross
M. Shearer
Peter Shellard
Alan Shelley
Leslie Sherlock
Stanley Shoop

Paul Sieveking
Louis Simmonds
Mrs. M. I. Simpson
Frank Smith
H. Smith of Liverpool Central Library
Helen Smith
Harold Smith
Timothy D'Arch Smith
Richard Spafford
I. G. Sparkes
D. Spector
Speleobooks
J. R. Sperr
John Spiers
David Stagg
Brian Staples
Martin Steenson
Andrew Stewart
Colin Stillwell
Christine Stockwell
G. E. C. and R. N. Stone
Martin Stone
Derek and Carol Summers
Robin Summers
Mitchell Symons
Nigel Tattersfield
Phil Thredder
Brian Tomes
Jeff Towns
M. Treloar
Triangle
Christine Trollope
Dr. R. J. Tunbridge
Morris Venables
Judi Vernau
David Wallechinsky
John Walton
Philip Ward
David Watkin
Susan Watkin
Steve Weissman
Robert Weissner
Bruce Whiteman
Anabelle Whittet

Avril Whittle
Nicholas Willmott
Alan Wilson
Philip Wilson
Gerry Wolstenholme
Charles B. Wood III
Les Wray
Robin Wright
Vivian Wright
Stephen Wycherley
Michael Zinman

*And our apologies to anyone
inadvertently omitted.*

BIZARRE INDEX